The Ravings of a Madman

The Ravings Of A Madman

Camino Elgarc

To order additional copies of this book, contact:
Xlibris
AU TFN: 1 800 844 927 (Toll Free inside Australia)
AU Local: (02) 8310 8187 (+61 2 8310 8187 from outside Australia)
www.Xlibris.com.au
Orders@Xlibris.com.au
842991

CONTENTS

To My Father

This is for all his strength, support, and generosity of spirit throughout my life and, in particular, during the times depicted in this book. He stood by me at a very difficult time in my life, offering hope and peace when chaos fell upon me.

My father died some months after my separation from my wife. Regrettably, he bore the brunt of my brutality during these times.

'Padre. Lo siento muchisimo. Perdoname.'

'Te quiero mucho.'

'Siempre.'

To My Children

They survived the events depicted in this book in their characteristically cheerful, supportive, loving way. They gave me purpose during dark times when all seemed lost and, in so doing, allowed me to reconnect to them and to life itself.

Introduction

What you are about to read is dark and confronting. It represents a period, long gone, when my life collapsed, and I had no answers. A lack of purpose and immense grief pushed me into a marginal existence where life itself became irrelevant and, at times, I imagined death as offering the only release from pain.

This is not uncommon; many people will have been through similar circumstances. Most survive, and I am one of them.

When I gave my draft to a good friend of mine for advice and comments, she suggested that I write an introduction that showed that I had come through these events and that I had prospered. I have. At the time, I saw no way through. I didn't care to find a way through. Psychoanalysis and associated drugs as well as support from friends allowed a thinning of clouds over time. I do not believe my mind would have allowed me to rest without the release of medication, and I do not believe medication would have been an option without professional help. In a situation such as that depicted here, drugs offer a small clearance of light in a world of shadows.

However, at the same time, I believe that trauma has a function. It slaps you in the face with a realignment of values that sometimes leads to growth – a growth partnered by change at a time when all your focus is on keeping things together, batting down the hatches to allow you to weather the storm. When the storm passes, you find a new you. The first thing to suffer was business. Not only did I not care about it, but also, I held it partly responsible for some of the damage to my family. I was very fortunate to have some people who continued to grind away at their job, who offered support in the best way they knew how – by doing their job. It somehow survived though substantially diminished. I have never again really worked at it. The new me did not have the capacity for prolonged effort, and I became a person of 'projects'. Most were purely indulgent, others for gain. Enough have succeeded so that I do not have an empty box awaiting a tick. I have done OK.

Bitterness at times entered my being. Thankfully, it did not stay. Unavoidably, it colours your perception and, consequently, your decisions. Decisions made in bitterness are seldom good decisions and mostly lead to further heartache. That is the first thing to purge. Memories of its existence remain in the scars of wounds from the past. Most of us carry emotional burdens from the battles of life and have built justifiable resistance towards taking on anymore. This is one of those.

What you are about to read is not a story of dread but of survival.

I had used a micro tape to record ideas for work when driving in my car, visiting businesses, or brainstorming with employees. When Sarah first left me, I found myself talking out loud to myself. I carried on discussions, being both proponent and devil's advocate. This was a form of release, a safety valve for an explosive mind, a mind in aggressive hostility with itself. Turmoil raged in my head. I needed to talk to someone, anyone, to discuss, analyse, plan for advice, someone who not only was impartial but also had my best interests at heart, someone who had my family's best interests at heart. I knew no one suitable. Most people I knew shied away from my obvious pain. They seemed embarrassed by my outpouring of grief. I had neither the strength to control my emotions nor the inclination to pretend otherwise. I could not keep a lid on my feelings; all systems were on overload. I feared the consequences of attempting to 'take control', and in any case, there was no way I could, even if I tried.

I have no family in Perth and missed the capacity to unburden or take counsel from people I love and trust and whose loyalty and love of me was unquestionable. I was very much alone in a crisis I had never anticipated and for which I had little experience. Sure, I had had previous relationship fallouts, with consequent pain, but this was in a totally different league. My family, my wife, and my life itself were on the line. As I faced the precipice, I clutched at anything that would help me from falling.

I phoned my sisters in Sydney. They too were taken by surprise. They offered advice and comforting words, but they were far removed from my current circumstances, both physically and emotionally. Though willing, they were powerless to help.

I soon came upon the idea of recording my ravings. Whilst not as good as talking to another human being, it was better than talking to thin air; God knows I had done enough of that. The little black recorder took on a life greater than its composite metal and plastic. It was my companion, always ready to listen, my black friend, a true friend, from whom I would keep no secrets. Always by my side, it would not betray me, it would never leave me, it did not have its own agenda, and most importantly, it would not judge me. I had lost confidence in people's capacity to understand my perspective and, therefore, their capacity to offer advice. If they had not walked in my shoes, how could they understand me or offer advice? Finally, I could talk into the black box freely, knowing that it would never betray my confidence.

Having the recorder with me at all times allowed me to record my thoughts as they occurred rather than trying to remember my feelings at a later stage. I could not believe that the life I had shared with Sarah was at an end. I was sure that Sarah and I would soon be discussing our future together, and I wanted her to know my feelings and to help her understand me. The best way to retell to her how I felt was if I could recall them, and I could not trust memory. I felt a strong need to record spontaneous feelings of loss, anger, fear, and pain as they happened and as I felt them at the time rather than commit them to an unreliable memory, coloured by later events.

Sarah had never previously behaved in the manner outlined below, and I immediately sensed that this was a metamorphic process in which we had embarked, a process that needed to be recorded. I hoped for a butterfly and feared a cockroach.

Initially, I had hoped that I'd be able to play it back to Sarah at a later stage, after we had forgiven each other, to show her how much I loved her. We would use the unadulterated recordings as one of the foundation stones upon to build our new life together. At that stage, I could not imagine life without Sarah. I was certain that we would resolve our differences within a reasonably short time. My references to finality at the time were, to a great extent, posturing. I could not believe she and I would not grow old together, see our children grow together, enjoy grandchildren together. I was as certain of her love for me as I was of mine for her and believed that she and I would work through this hurdle in our life and move on. Numerous discussions with Sarah had confirmed the 'foreverness' of our lives together. Our future was to be shared. We were meant to be.

Subconsciously though, I was probably giving myself a warning of the possibility of something I had not previously considered – that perhaps she had decided on a life without me and our life together was over. That which had previously been unforeseen was indeed possible. Out of left field, my future may suddenly change. Strange to think that something that has yet to happen, our future, could change. Of course, that which has not happened does not change. What changes is our predictions of what is likely to happen, and all my previous predictions were now under siege.

I found that by using the tape recorder to put into words my thoughts and feelings, I was better able to make sense of the potpourri of emotions playing havoc with my head and heart – not that I often replayed them, for that would create a crescendo of pain whose whirlpool would draw me further into a quagmire from which release became more difficult. Rather, the mere fact of speaking and recording eased the angst in my soul. This self-analysis became immediately useful when attempting to enlist the help of others in my quest to find Sarah and my children or to have others help us build bridges that I hoped would eventually bring us back together.

Sarah had taken my three children and placed a restraining order to prevent me from attempting to see them. As the hearing date to my efforts to lift the restraining order neared, the recorder was particularly useful. It helped to structure my approach/strategy with solicitors, to anchor my thoughts/ feelings, and to prepare me for fronting a magistrate who would rule whether and when I could see my children again. I needed an anchor to steady the storm in my head, to structure my thoughts when terror, chaos, and destruction ruled my being. In doing so, the recorder helped to ease my fears of an uncertain outcome by some very small degree.

I first used the tape on the Monday night in which I was served with the restraining order. This restraint came to me as a great shock. It was not something I ever expected from the person I loved – totally out of left field, a strategic death blow. I had viewed it as something that other people use against uncontrollable misfits who endanger those around them, a weapon of State to be used against low-lives who abuse their wives and children and who need State intervention to control their lack of humanity. I would have never thought that a restraining order would be requested, let alone granted, on someone like me. I felt deeply ashamed of having been served with a restraining order and could not discuss it with anyone. I was at odds as to how I would be able to explain a restraining order to anyone. I had always imagined it being taken out to restrain abusive low-lives and feared everyone would share my opinion of them. How would I be able to explain such a thing to anyone?

The night of shame was long. It was not until the following day, after having visited our local police station and discussing it with the duty sergeant, that I was able to deal with my shame. Robin was my best friend at the time, and it was he who first heard that Sarah had placed a restraining order on me. He was witness to my relationship with my children as well as the occasional argument with Sarah. As such, I was confident that he would recognise that I was not the sort of vile person who needed a restraining order and felt he was best able to judge whether or not I was a beast. I needed to tell someone, and he seemed to me the best person with whom to discuss my shame. As I told him, I sensed his eyes upon me, seeking any hints that may betray a previously unknown trait in my character. He watched me closely and assessed my answers for clues of previously undetected brutality.

My first use of the tape required that I recount events from the previous few days. This has the note of storytelling and lacks spontaneity. It also relies on the memory of a mind on overload and less than capable of prioritising or coherent recollection. It is muddled and stifled. I turned it on to live recordings on the Monday after having answered the door to two police officers who had served a restraining order on me. I sat at the kitchen table and turned it on. From then, I recorded as the thoughts and feelings came to me. I could speak truthfully; I did not edit them or attempt to pasteurise them as they were not going to be heard by anyone other than me. Perhaps Sarah would also hear them at a later stage, but by then, we would be reconciled and friends again. She would not judge then harshly.

I allowed my mind, in extreme turmoil, to throw up anything it wanted to and in any order it saw fit without concern for peer/social control. Anger, fear, and pain coloured my thoughts. Thoughts bubbled and burst out of control. My mind darted from one thought to the next, often without resolution, returning to it at a later day for reassessment. As a result, some thoughts recur, and certain issues are repeated throughout the text as my mind tried to make sense with them. I contradicted myself, argued from different perspectives, and oftentimes had a complete reversal of opinion. They represent the workings of a deeply troubled mind.

Soon, talking into the tape became a very natural process for me. Whenever possible, I recorded major thoughts, mood changes, breakthroughs, and other significant events as they occurred, sometimes in the middle of the night, when I awoke to a darkness filled with terror and regrets. In some of my recordings, I would scream in anger at the machine. In others, my whispers would be almost inaudible, especially when whispering through tears. Playing back these tapes, I would, at times, find it very difficult to understand what I had said.

My little black friend was always with me. I took it in the car, had it on my desk at work, by my bed table when I tried, with varying degrees of success, to sleep at night.

Revisiting these recordings was a struggle. It rekindled many forgotten feelings I had experienced way back when, in a previous life; I was a husband and a father.

The Players

Sarah:	My wife of eighteen years
Claudia:	Our 7-year-old daughter
Jessica:	Our 5-year-old daughter
Ben:	Our 3-year-old son
Taroo:	Our 12-year-old Boxer bitch, the family dog
Robin Abramovich:	My best friend (his family and my family were best friends; we did many things together as families)
Laura Abramovich:	Robin's wife, a good friend of Sarah's
Mary:	My elder sister (two and a half years older)
Patricia:	My younger sister (two and a half years younger)
Yayi:	'Granddad', my father
Albert Clinsman:	Sarah's father
Rachel Clinsman:	Sarah's mother
Donna:	My secretary
Don Hughes:	A Sydney friend
Peter Burton:	Mutual friend, lives in Perth but also from Sydney
Belinda:	Our neighbour, Sarah's friend
Susie:	Belinda's daughter
Janice, Joan Burton, and Julie:	Sarah's friends
Roy Ness,	

John Oldfield,
Giselle,
Jean and Dale
Wakefield,
Michael and Debbie
Court,
Tim and Phillipa
Vautier,
the Heatons, Daniel,
Sally and Robert
McCormish,
and Alison Johnson: All mutual friends
Robert Howard: President of my rotary club
Jake Carlino: My solicitor (I have known Jake for quite some time; we were both seniors in aikido and had trained together for many years)
Black Know-all   My micro recorder

Tape 1

Betrayal and Destruction

Monday night, at home, four days into the fire

When she first left me, I felt anger – clear, white anger at her for taking Claudia away, taking Jessica and taking Ben away. She had stolen my children.

Betrayal. Whilst I was away at work, working for all of us, she had plotted. She had gathered her toiletries, packed a few other things – small, trivial nothings – and gone. I felt totally betrayed. I too had been angry with her and depressed over our argument. I too could have gone away. But I stayed. I went to work and came home. I stayed for us. I didn't run away.

Claudia had invited Susie for a sleepover. She had been overjoyed on Thursday, planning for her and Susie to cook a pizza for us, the family, on Friday night. I was looking forward to sharing her joy. I had hoped that her infectious joy would allow Sarah and me the opportunity to bridge our differences and make up.

I came home to an empty house.

Distraught and betrayed, I drove to different people's houses, hoping to find her. I went to Laura's place, Jean's, Giselle's, and the court. She was nowhere to be seen. Exhausted, I returned home and tried to sleep. With little success.

On Saturday, I woke up angry. I was angry at the violation. Robin helped me through that. He kept reassuring me that she was all right and would be back as soon as she cooled down. I was expecting her to return at any time. I didn't go to aikido as I normally do on Saturdays. I thought that she would return at that time, taking the opportunity to collect a few other essentials whilst expecting me not to be there. All day, I spent racing to the front window whenever I heard a noise, expecting it to be her return.

The following day, Sunday, anger was replaced by sadness. Sadness enveloped me completely. My pores oozed doom. I was sad, immobilised by fear, as my mind raced from one disastrous consequence to another without analysis or understanding. Demons ruled my mind, a mind short-circuiting into chaos.

We had arranged to have a few people over to play a game of 'diplomacy'. The previous day, I had considered cancelling it but decided against it. I wasn't up to fielding questions, the answers to which I didn't know. Besides, I'd hoped she'd be back by then. So I pretended everything was normal. Jack, Sue, Jim, Dean, and two of my aikido students, Jim, and Simon, came over and played. When they asked about Sarah and the children, I answered that Sarah had taken the children away for the day. This was, in part, true.

I expected her to turn up at any time. After the game, we went to a nearby pub and played pool and drank lots. Afterward, Jim and Dean came back home with me. The alcohol weakened my defences to contain my secret. I could no longer keep it inside. I put on Hendrix's 'Machine Gun' at full bore and cried as Jim and Dean consoled me.

On Monday, I still hoped that she would be back when I returned from work. I came home hoping to see her there, but the place was empty still.

It was then I decided I needed to act rather than just wait expectantly for her return. It was very serious, and there was no longer any point in pretending that nothing was wrong. I began contacting everyone we both knew, hoping to get some clues as to her whereabouts. The simple act of trying to contact people proved to be difficult as she had taken the Teledex and I didn't have any phone numbers. I found many of our friends' phone numbers in the white pages. My search was often futile as there were many people whom we knew only by first names. I began by listing all the people to whom she was close and who were not close to me. Could she be with Phillipa? Not having her phone number, I drove down to Mosman Park and looked around outside her house for signs of Sarah and the children. Nothing.

This morning, Monday, I drove around the hills, looking for Julie. I didn't know her address. I'd only been there once. I drove around unfamiliar streets, looking for anything recognisable, without success. Tonight I drove again around the hills and was successful in finding Julie's place. I was pleased with myself at having found the house as every house looked the same at night. I knocked on the door and was greeted with surprise, went in, and asked about her. She wasn't there. They didn't know anything and seemed genuinely surprised by her actions.

Tonight I was served with . . . a restraining order. I heard a noise by the door, and I went to open it, hoping to find Sarah there. Instead, there were two police officers asking for me. A restraining order. She has put a restraint on me that prevents me from seeing her and my children. I'm not permitted to see my children. The restraining order is an 'interim' order until the hearing date, on 10 March.

That's so far away. I can't not see my children for that long. How can I live that long without them?

I'm restrained from 'striking, touching, or entering any premises occupied by the complainant'. She has served me with a restraining order on behalf of my children. I'm not allowed to be in the same place as Claudia . . . Ben . . . or Jessica. I'm restrained from seeing *my* children.

I don't understand . . . I don't understand how these things happen. This strikes at the core of my being. Where is my purpose? If I don't have a family, what am I doing? What is the purpose of this life?

———

I surrender everything. She has won. Her betrayal ensured her victory before a shot was fired. She has stolen my children. I don't want anything. The end. Please, Sarah. Call this off. I surrender.

Can it be fixed? If I submit completely, can it be fixed? And if it can, where is my strength? Where is my reason for doing things? For living?

I thought we had a good marriage. I took pride, pride in our marriage. There are all these outsiders involved now, all these people who think our marriage is touchy, shaky, which it obviously is.

I didn't know.

Sides. They take sides. It's remarkable they take sides. They stonewall me for the sake of her friendship. *Fools!* What are you doing? I'm fighting for my family. I'm trying to get in contact with her to, I don't know . . . talk . . . I don't care. Anything.

I know she's well. Feedback from people that have spoken to her tell me she is well. I hope so.

I just want to talk. She hasn't contacted me. I don't know where she is. She might be with the Burtons, but I don't know their phone number. They've moved, and I don't know where they live now, so I can't get their phone number from the white pages.

I get a cold reception from unexpected quarters. Cold reception. 'Oh yes, well, can I pass on a message?' *Pass on a message?* They're my children. Wake up. They are my children. What gives? What gives one person the right, *absolute* right, over our children? She takes them – she takes them, and they are hers. And I'm prevented from seeing them. *Bastards!*

My children. Our children. They would be asking, 'Where is Daddy?' They would be missing me, wanting me.

I would do anything to reverse this. I don't want to score points. It is too dangerous to play mind games. The stakes are too high. My children and my marriage are on the line. I'd do anything to stop this.

Have we done irreparable damage? That which was the source of my strength, that which kept me going, dealing with all sorts of bastards, witness to cruelty and savagery. Is it gone? That which gave me the strength to fight on in the comfort that I have a happy family, children I love and who love me, a wife that I love and who loves *me*. I belong to them and they to me. Is that all gone?

I've never fucked around with anybody. I have had no affairs. I don't do that.

My family is . . . My family is my all.

I feel so betrayed.

But I don't want recompense for betrayal. It doesn't matter. It doesn't matter now. I would like things to be what I thought they were. Which they obviously were not. I was wrong, delusional. And . . . I will do anything required. She can have the house. She can live here, and I'll move away.

Outside forces encroach on my family. Society determines. A piece of paper restrains me from seeing my children. What right does anyone have to prevent me from seeing my children? They are mine, and I am theirs. It's my blood that flows through their veins. Me and them. Us.

Can it ever be fixed? Would I . . . would I forgive . . . someone . . . for doing this to me? I would . . . I think! She's my wife, the mother of my children. And I love her. I don't know how not to love her.

The foundation upon which . . . my persona, my *me* is based is . . . wrong. I don't have a happy family. I have a family that is so sick . . . that one of its participants, my wife, feels she needs to go to the police and restrain me from seeing my children.

She fears me. *She fears me.* How can she fear me? We are one.

They are my children. They need me. Do they love me or just need me? Both . . . I think . . . No! I know that my little gorgeouses love *and* need me.

I love them a lot. I love them. I do – lots. God . . . I'm very, very lonely.

Aaaaahhhhh!

Aaaaaaaaaaahhhhh!

How could she do this to me? I gave away friendships. I hardly keep in contact with people. Sarah is the go-between. I'm a recluse. I overdose so much on people in my work. Home is my refuge. I see such a lot of the worst in people. Greed, cruelty, lack of empathy. When I can, I withdraw. I'm complete with my family. Everybody else is superfluous. Other people are of no consequence. I have contacts with lots of people. I'm sociable, but only my family matters. I'm happy to go and have fish and chips at Fremantle with them. Anything. *Just us.* I don't need anyone else. *I need my family.*

It must be me. My sisters are not like this. They can write off family members easily. I've always had a sense of my place in the family, ancestors, descendants, etc. Maybe being the only boy, with two sisters, has affected me. Maybe my cultural backgrounds . . . *Fuck!* What the *fuck* do I know?

Is this out of place? Do these values no longer apply? Am I such a dinosaur? And if I am, how do I change? Do I want to change anyway? Yes, I would, for my family. I would. I will.

My little boy . . . my son. Ben, where are you? Where are you, my gorgeous?

Ben . . . You hardly know me. Three years young. Are you to grow up without your father?

If you won't know me, how will you understand me? How will we share values? I *don't* want to be a stranger. I'm your *father.* Your father. I love you.

Is she falling out of love with me? Is she coming to the conclusion to stay away? How can she leave and not write me a note? Or ring me? To tell me 'I don't want to see you', 'I don't want you to see me', 'I'm going to be away for a week, two weeks', whatever? To let me know? Just to let me know? A fucking lousy note, that's all. A note.

My children. Where are they?

Is she falling out of love? After all the crying, will she decide that she no longer loves me? If that happens, what do I do? What do I do? I don't want to hurt the children. Claudia . . . my lovely, lovely Claudia. Beautiful Jessica and little Ben. What do I do? What do I do? Do I simply forget about them? Can I forget them and love them? And I think . . . Do I fight for them? Fight . . . Go to court and have some clown make a decision on my family. And possibly lose anyway. Do I . . . do I give it up and say, 'OK, OK, you take the kids. Fine. I'll just disappear'?

***

How can I live without them? What is there to do? What? Why?

Why live?

Do I start again? Do I find some other woman, whom I don't know, and have other children?

I don't want other children. I want Claudia, Jessica, and Ben. I don't want other children. I already have three children that I love, and I think, know, they love me. So why can someone unilaterally dismember my family? I would never, *never* take them away from her – *never.* I wouldn't do such a thing.

Whatever the problem, I would tough it out with her some way. Work it out, work through it, I don't know. Maybe that's because I'm such a hard bastard and she fears me. Domineering. But I would never take Jessica, Ben, and Claudia from their mommy. So how come Mommy can take Jessica, Ben, and Claudia from their daddy? Or to take their daddy away from them? If this has got to be the case . . . I . . .

No! I'm still optimistic. I play with options, but I really do not . . . *I do not* . . . believe my marriage is finished. I don't want my marriage to fail.

I do not want to see my children every second weekend. That's ridiculous. I'm optimistic that we can solve it, whatever *it* is. We must solve this . . . whatever. But it's peculiar that events would unfold as they have. This is

7

very atypical of Sarah. She is usually very considerate. She's such a good woman. What has happened to her? To us?

There is no system for resolution. Everyone runs for cover. No one steps in and decides to help. They're all too scared . . . of getting involved. And I'm a wife beater from now on . . . or a child molester, someone that needs to be restrained. That stigma will remain. I've had a restraining order placed on me by my wife. My wife fears for her safety to the extent that she has gone to God knows where, and the only contact I've had from her has been by way of police knocking on my door . . . Restraint.

'Criminal psychopath, you cannot be trusted. I'm restraining you, you dog.'

When I heard the car, my heart skipped a beat, ever hopeful that she is coming back to me. But if she doesn't even ring, I doubt if she would just turn up. She's too scared to see me. I hear some movement outside, and my expectations rise, thinking she is at the door.

I surrender. I'm not prepared to risk the consequences. I want to move away from the brink. I don't want to fall. I'm scared. I want to come away from the brink. I want to come away from the brink, and I want to forget there ever was a brink. I want to be able to . . .

Are Sarah's and my values so different? Are we not friends? My friend. My friend Sarah with whom I shared many, most things. She's my friend. Are we, are our opinions so different? Moving away without leaving a note – would I do that? Our family is in crisis. Where is the commonality? She's my friend.

And . . . why? Why did it go like this? Why did it go like this?

The privacy of my own home is shattered. A man's home is his castle. I close the door at night, and the world stays outside. No longer. The world is crashing in and raping my home and me. And it is Sarah that has sent the rapists in. I wouldn't have contacted anybody. I would have hoped that we could sort this out without everybody knowing that we had a problem. I didn't know we had such a big problem . . . Obviously.

———

Fool. You're a fucking idiot, Garc. But . . .

I have had no phone calls, no note, nothing . . . After one day, I had to contact people just to find out how she was or where she was. To see if I can get her back. And . . . see if there is anything that can be done. No secrets. Now everybody knows, and people have taken sides.

So what happens in two months' time, in three months' time, when we go and visit these people, if . . . God, please . . . not if, when . . . when . . . when we repair this? They will know that our marriage is shaky. And I know it is shaky. I didn't know . . . I didn't know. I didn't think it was. Not perfect, but good. *I didn't know.*

Idiot!

Who gives a fuck what they think?

Today I rang up Robert Howard and told him, and he gave me the suggestion of a marriage counselling service. A suggestion. At last, advice. That's what I was going to do. But Sarah goes to the police and puts a restraining order on me. She goes to the *police.*

The world is no longer outside my door. The door has been kicked in. There is no haven for me. I am exposed to the world . . . bleeding in public.

Where is she?

Is she crying?

I don't want her to . . . to cry me away.

The children need us. I need them. I need . . . her. I love her. I love her. I don't understand this. We've done so much together. Eighteen years. Is it eighteen? I was 24 . . . I'm . . . My mind is not functioning . . . I can't add up. Eighteen years, yes. Eighteen years.

Dylan, did you know Sarah? 'Sad-eyed Sarah, beautiful lady so dear to my heart'?

I don't want this. I can't understand how . . .

She no longer loves me. How? How can I bring her back? It's all . . . too dangerous.

I don't want us to become another statistic. 'Children of a broken marriage'. I don't want a broken marriage, even without the children. I love her. I need her. She's been my friend, my love. I don't know how to exist without her, without my beautiful chil . . .

I remember ten years ago, talking to Don Hughes before moving to Perth and saying that I'd been dealt a bad hand and that I'd kept my ace and thrown in all my other cards. Sarah was my ace. I came here to Perth with nothing but Sarah. I still feel the same. She's the most important part in my life, and I don't think we should break that which is so precious to us both.

How can I not see my children until after 10 March? How can someone restrain a father from seeing his children? On the strength of unanswered accusations, some fool can place a restraining order on me and prevent me from seeing *my* children for three weeks. I can't see my children for more than three weeks. It's a cruel turn. Too cruel.

This is a fucking outrage.

I don't know why she's done this. She should love me. As I love her.

I ache.

It's really hard not to go into self-destruct. It is hard to stop myself from doing destructive things. Sometimes, when I'm driving in my car and heading towards another car, there is an urge not to swerve and to smash against it. Or at an intersection, instead of giving way, I feel like driving through, in the hope of getting wiped out. It would be a release to have a fatal accident. My mind is full of thoughts of self-destruction. It won't leave me.

Day 5, — Tuesday, 10:40, in my office

Still no contact, no call, no note. I'm going fucking crazy. My mind is thrashing about, out of control. Panic – in uncontrollable and incomprehensible flight.

I've been in contact with Peter Burton, and he seemed surprised that Sarah has left me, so I don't think she is with them. I'm going to try the Heatons and Alison Johnson. I'm running out of options.

Where is she?

I don't want to get on to Jake and start the merry-go-round of hostilities with lawyers and the like. Even though she has engaged the services of the State to restrain me from seeing my children. Bitch. I don't believe that will get us anywhere. Lawyers. It's too early to engage undertakers.

We are in a metamorphic process. Things can never be the same. I hope that the change can be for the better though . . . I didn't understand it to be so late, that we were so far apart. And I hope that the change is one that . . . that I can cope with, live with, one that lasts . . . so my family is not destroyed. I hope . . . but I don't know what Sarah hopes or feels. I hope in a vacuum. I don't know how this has happened. That she can take it so far. Or how much further she is prepared to go.

I surrender. I surrender. I don't care. I give up. Please, Sarah. Break off hostilities. Please.

In the car

Another useless journey. Her car is not at the Heatons'. Her car doesn't appear to be at the Heaton's' place.

Is she with Alison? I don't know. I'll have to drive there to see.

I'm becoming a menace on the road, taking up too much room, stopping suddenly, driving too fast/slow, turning unpredictably, not indicating, and going into strangers' driveways for no reason. All the time talking to you, my small black friend. I must appear a lunatic. At the moment, I probably am one.

Back in my office

Has she met someone? Has she met someone that is going to replace me? Someone who will come to be my children's father?

Aaaaahhhhh! Cunt.

She's a *cunt*. I don't know this woman . . . this woman that has taken my children . . . without letting me know . . . where? For how long? Without calling me and without leaving me a note. I don't know her. I don't know this woman who sets the police on to me either. The Sarah I know would never have done this. The Sarah I know is not cruel. These aren't two people, so the Sarah I know doesn't exist. I do not know Sarah. Did I invent her? Does she only exist in my mind? Surely not. Am I that blind? That stupid? Sarah, my Sarah, does not exist. Did I make her up? Surely not. Have I? What do I do about that? How do I handle being in love with someone that doesn't exist?

Who is this woman? *Who is this woman?*

Who am I? Who am I, to have done whatever it is that I have done to have caused this woman to behave in a way that I don't recognise? Who is she? And what do I do about that? What do I do? Where do I go from here? Where is my supportive friend? Where is *she*? Why won't *she* call me? Why doesn't she call me? Why doesn't she cast away this other cruel stranger and call me? Resurface, please, Sarah, and get rid of this bastard that is killing me and destroying us. Please come quickly. Time is not on our side. Sarah, where are you? She is destroying our family. Resurface, my love. Resurface, please. Save us.

Why am I talking to this machine? Why am I taping my lunacy? What comfort do I get by talking into a stupid micro tape? Why blab my all into this little black box? Who will ever listen to you anyway? You are a *fucking idiot*, Garc. No wonder you're in such a mess. Hopefully, no one will ever hear you except for me. Or maybe Sarah will hear it and understand me. Or maybe, if everything goes wrong, someone else can hear it. But why? Why should I care about that? What sicko reasons do I have for talking to you?

Who gives a fuck?

I give a fuck. My soul is evaporating.

Is it because I find it difficult to express myself, to get my thoughts in order, coherently? Could it be that I'm hoping that by taping my scramble, I will not miss anything important? Why record? Why am I telling all my secrets to an inanimate black box that can offer me no advice? Is that the reason? If you offer no advice, you offer no opinion, make no judgement. Is this it? Am I talking to someone without letting anyone in on my secrets?

Late afternoon in my car

I'm clutching at straws. I'm clutching . . . at straws. Looking for her in places I know she is unlikely to be. But any chance is a chance worth taking. In any case, she's behaving in an unpredictable way, so I have to look where I don't expect. I'm clutching at straws. I mean, why would she go to Alison's place? She hasn't gone to Julie's, the Heatons. She's not with the Abramoviches. Where is she?

I've been in contact with lots and lots of people now. I've visited everyone I can think of. I have no choice. I have to look for her. I have told many people. Many people know. I hope she contacts one or any number of them and they . . . they tell her . . . that I want to talk to her and that she decides to talk to me.

I've done more miles in the last three days, four days, and five days than I have in months and months. Man! More than the last five months put together.

I don't recognise any house in Johnson Street as being that of Alison. I drive down the street parallel to Johnson Street, and I don't recognise anything.

The courts appear to be mostly one-sided. I'll try them again, and I'll try everybody in North Perth again, and then I'll go to Janice's place, the Abramoviches. Then I'll have to speak to Jake. I'm going to have to get on to a solicitor to try to get my family back. And I know it won't work. I just know . . . that won't work. Accusations and hostility and further damage.

Who does she know that would keep her and three children secretly for that long? Keep them all for so long? Who is so close? So close to them, my children, that she can rely on them when she's taken my children and left me? Who? Who? And I don't know them. Who are they? Think, Garc! It must be obvious. Think! Who are these people?

Evening in my car

I'm outside of Panetta's house. She's not here.

I'm restrained from seeing my children. The school must also know. 'Deviant father might sneak up and steal the children. Beware of the beast.' I'm driving around the school hoping that she is there. Why would she be there? But what else is there to do?

Needless to say, there is no one near the school.

Did she decide to put a restraining order on me by herself? Was she so emotionally upset? Was someone else involved in advising her? Who does these sorts of things?

If my kids are happy and contented so far, as Laura claims Sarah said, where are they? They must be with other kids to be so happy. Someone with a swimming pool or a holiday place. That's why I thought of Julie and the Burtons. They have children, Brigitte and Kate, and a swimming pool. 'Sarah says.' Of course, she says that. What else can she say? That the children are miserable, that they miss their father, that what she has done is selfish and brutal, that she has made a huge mistake? 'Happy and contented', my fucking arse.

There's no one at Jean's place. 'Time keeps on ticking, ticking, into the future.' So goes the song. And as it does, it becomes increasingly difficult to repair the damage. Tick, tick, fucking tick.

It's unspeakably frustrating that I haven't been able to figure out where she is. Where is she? How can I not know where she is? She needs to take the kids to school, so she must be nearby. She is taking the kids to school. I think I know that. I think someone told me. Do I really know? Am I making it up? Fuck. My mind is playing tricks on me. I'm not sure now. If she is not taking the children to school, she could be anywhere. But she has been able to visit people in North Perth, City Beach, so she can't be too far away. No. She must be near. I think she is nearby.

What am I doing, wracking my brain, trying to decipher this painful puzzle without clues? Why can't I relax and let it pass over me, block out until something turns up? This is futile. I should go into pain block, try to forget everything. Block out. Denial. Put it aside until it passes or I am better able to deal with it. Nothing is working anyway. I'm not getting anywhere.

No! No, I won't. I want to feel. I want to burn with feeling. I don't want nothingness. What I'm doing is not futile. *It is not futile*. I'm trying as best I know to find my wife and children. It is not futile . . .

It's not effective. So far, I have had nothing but failure and a lot of waste . . . so far, a waste of time and effort, unsuccessful but not futile. I have to try . . . I cannot give up . . . I will not, in the future, look back on this. If I fail and continue to fail, I . . . I must not be able to look back on this with regret at not having tried hard enough when it really mattered. I must keep trying. With success or failure, I have to keep trying and hope that I stumble upon something that gives me a break. I don't want guilt of having acted half-baked at the wrong time. Is that it? Am I doing this for myself? Am I acting for the future? I don't think I'm doing this to appease my conscience. God knows that my conscience is troubled and will need to

———

pay its dues for a long time to come. My conscience is anything but clear. I have regrets over so many things. But this has nothing to do with fault.

I'm not saying that in the future, I will be able to say it was not my fault because obviously, it is. But I'm trying. I try. I'm trying as best I can. And . . . and maybe I'll get lucky.

Maybe I'll get lucky.

As I drive around, I look around to see if I can spot her car. Ha! Ridiculous. Needle in haystack stuff.

She could be with one of the Dodgey Brother types, but I don't know of anyone she is close enough to. Is there anyone that she is close to? Paula? No! No, Dick wouldn't wear it. The Oldfields? She'd be fucking sick and tired of them by now. The children wouldn't be happy there. Maybe . . . maybe McCormish? With Sally and Robert. He's a kind person, accommodating. She and Sally get on. Sort of. Maybe. Oh, I don't know. Fuck! I don't think so. This is stupid.

Who else is there? Think, Garc, think.

I hope I can forgive those that have acted against my family and me. Those that have taken sides to the extent that they have interfered with my attempts to get in contact with my wife and family. Out of loyalty to Sarah? Is that enough? Can I forgive such short-sightedness?

I'm driving up to Laura's place, and fuck! My heart's in my throat. Laura is at work. Ha! She's not at Laura's place. Robin's car is there. Robin, who 'loves me like a brother'.

I've been an arsehole lately, I suppose. Mistreating my father. I've always been a bit of an arsehole, but lately, I've been much worse. More – yes, more – of an arsehole. Less sensitive, more hostile, domineering, intransigent. An absolute cunt, I suppose.

I'm now driving to Elsa's place. She is a good friend of Sarah. Dale, her husband, and I were just beginning to become friends. But Elsa rules the roost, and she is very much *Sarah's* friend, so I don't hold much hope for that friendship. If she is there, it would only be for a visit. She wasn't there on Sunday. I know that. I drove around and saw Dale. I don't think he saw me. I didn't want to be seen. My hope, slim as it is, is that she's there, visiting. Visiting. Ha! A half hour's visit in a whole day to coincide with me going there. What are the chances of that, even if she has visited? Straws.

The place is empty. There's no one here, and I have nowhere else to try.

You, black know-all – what are *your* opinions of me? So far, my ramblings have been full of self-doubt and pity. Defeated etc. I . . . Obviously, self-doubt is very much at the forefront of all my thoughts. But I now know that I don't want to be angry . . . I don't want to be angry. I don't think that being angry is going to help. I want to clear my mind and let it concentrate on repair and nothing else. Flush out from my mind the destruction of anger. You are helping me. Your non-judgemental silence is allowing me to unravel the chaos in my mind. Help me, little one. Don't give up on me.

I'm in the car again, off to pay a few bills for work etc. Then I'll head back to the office and hope that there is a message from someone, anyone, that may lead to a breakthrough.

At office

Nothing.

No news.

I hate going home at night to an empty house. I'd prefer to go anywhere but my empty house. I do so in the hope she'll ring. I don't want to miss her call if she rings. I patrol the front windows hoping to spot her first if . . . if she returns. I'm fucking exhausted. I haven't been sleeping. I have been staying awake as long as I can, hoping to get very tired so I can sleep. Then I sleep for a couple of hours, awaken, and cannot go back to sleep.

In my car

I have just thought of another prospect. She may be with Joan Burton. I really hope she's the one. I should have thought of her before. It seems so obvious now. But I didn't. In any case, I really, really hope she is there. For Christ's sake, please be there. And so I drive on from West Perth to Clarkson on a long shot. A very long shot. Thirty-five kilometres each way.

Each and every time I approach somewhere where I hope she is going to be, I . . . I just want her to be there so much. I lift. I become excited. I have all the things I want to say to her roll about intoxicatingly inside my mind. I so much want her to be there. Then I arrive, and she's not there, and I hit the pits again. This time may be different. I really hope that she's here. She should be here. I want her to be here. It makes sense that she be here.

There's so much I want to say. First and foremost, I want to say to her that I love her. To say, 'Let's not do this.' 'Let's choose not to do this.' But I don't know if she will listen, believe me, or whether she's turned, she's off somewhere else, on another wavelength. What will I do when I get there if she is not there? What will I do?

Outside Joan's house

There's no one here. The place is empty. I'll wait until someone comes home.

It's five twenty-five, and there's still no one at Joan's place. I've been suffering from heat exhaustion and have a headache from all the sun. All sand and no trees. There's no shade anywhere. I can't wait any longer. I must head off back home. I'm hoping that Laura has made contact with Sarah, and she'll have some news. I don't want to miss her call.

TAPE 2

The Institutional Destruction of Love

Day 6 — Wednesday, in the office

I feel as if I have been under a cloud of emotions that's affecting my views and killing my head and heart.

You, my small biographer, will note from my shaking voice that things haven't changed. You may even detect anger again in my voice. I was trying to suppress anger and find a resolution. Yet anger swells uncontrollably inside me. I want to be free of it, but my mind continues to bring forth evidence to support an angry stance. I'm tortured by thoughts of vengeance.

Until yesterday, I was prepared to submit. I think. And to do anything that she required so that we may begin to talk. Today things are different. Today I've stopped feeling sorry for myself. Today I don't feel comfortable with feeling sorry for myself. Today I think I'm more of a fighter than that. I'm not going to commit suicide. I'm not going to give it all up.

Self-pity is again replaced with feelings of betrayal and anger. I've been betrayed by the very someone whom I trusted most. She has put my family on the line for the sake of . . . I don't know what. I can no longer, no longer trust her. Yesterday I would have been prepared to, for the sake of the family, let it fade. But her silence and absence destroy the dwindling flame of hope.

I tried to talk to her, but she refused. She was at Robin's place, and unexpectedly, by a freak chance, I happened to call at that time. Phillip, Robin's son, answered the phone and told me she was there. I told Phillip to ask her to talk to me. Eventually, she came to the phone, but instead of talking to me, she took the phone from Phillip and hung up on me. She, who has stolen my children. My most precious thing. My family. And she has destroyed it. She fucking hung up on me without so much as a word. *Cunt.*

She took them when I was at work, completely defenceless. Didn't leave me a note, hasn't called me, will not respond to all the messages that I have left for her with anybody who cares enough to get involved. I've been forced to humiliate myself in front of everyone I know. Desperate . . . desperate attempts to locate her. I've cried in front of strangers. Embarrassed them and me with my pain. And she hangs up on me.

People view me with suspicion, assessing to see if I could be a Jekyll and Hyde. I appear a nice enough fellow, but what monster lurks hidden just below the surface? Some will have come to the conclusion that I am a wife beater and/or child molester. Otherwise, why would I have been restrained?

She's preventing me from seeing my children when she knows how much they mean to me. She's doing this to hurt me. She wants to hurt me. On purpose. I don't think I can live with any woman that has destroyed so much, so quickly, without warning. She's not the person I was in love with. So now I won't talk to her unless she lifts the restraining orders on me and brings back my children. Unless she does that, I have nothing to say to her. Today I'm taking off my wedding ring. I'm not going to let my business fold because of her. There are many beautiful women available. Maybe what I need is someone that . . . I don't know what I need. But I don't need someone that betrays me when I'm at my weakest. She's made my children suffer. I want to prevent that, but I don't think I can. I don't think I can help it any longer. She has changed circumstances. The rules of the game are very different. I wish, I wish we could turn back the clock. But we can't, and what sort of life would it be if she came back? Under what circumstances would it work? I don't know. I still hope that it does, but it cannot be a surrender, a complete capitulation by one party, me. It wouldn't work.

How much can I change anyway? I am me. I am prepared to change, but I need encouragement. She must meet me some of the way. It can't all be up to me. What about me? How much can I change anyway?

I demand that the fucking restraining order be lifted, and I demand to be able to see my children. If she won't do that, then I won't do any more.

Robin said that she was going to write to me. She can write to me, but I cannot write to her because I don't know where she is. She can ring me, but I can't ring her. She can come and see me, but she doesn't, and I can't see her. It's all too one-sided, too unfair. I was trying to hold back my anger, slow down the rush to the brink of destruction, but I don't know if I want to any longer. She's a bastard. She is a bastard.

I've spoken to Jake, and he tells me that this thing has all the hallmarks of being premeditated. He believes that a restraining order is consistent with that view. He has warned me that the next three months will be the most horrible time of my life. His opinion is both professional and based on personal experience. I believe him. I know that to be true. I'm prepared for it as much as anybody can be. He says that she must be at some sort of refuge for women. The restraining order could also result from this. Women's refuges, which he says are headed by man-hating lesbians, often use these tactics. They may have advised her. He has very extremist views. I'm trying to separate the advice from the opinion. The last thing I need is other people's prejudices clouding my judgement. I have told him that my objective is to save the marriage, if at all possible. He accepts that (though I feel that he believes it to be a hard ask). He has told me that the next step will be that I'll be issued with a letter of demand from a solicitor. Also possible is that I may be getting letters from the Family Court. He explained that she has probably gone before a magistrate one morning and has accused me of all sorts of things, about me being violent etc., that convinced a magistrate to put a restraining order on me, that she might have legal aid.

I'm told that on 10 March, we will front the court to say that we will defend the restraint and that the court will set a date for the hearing, which will be sometime in April, probably, by which time we will argue our case. He is confident that I will get access.

Access. Can you imagine? I'm going to get access to my children. Jake believes that she's very likely to get custody. Why her? Why not me? She betrays, not me. They are my children. How can she take them and condemn me to a life of solitude? Not alone but a father without children. How? How? They should be with me. I love them and do all for them. Jake says that bearing in mind that I am running a business, I would have to go into minute detail of what I do every second of my day to prove that I can look after the children. He says that employing a nanny would not sway the court in my favour. Keeping the business and asking for custody won't succeed. If I sell the business and stay home to look after my children, I will have to prove the means by which I will be able to support them. He's not hopeful of me getting up on that either. 'Catch-22'. What a fucking mess, with few options. Damned if I do, damned if I don't. Men are disposable. Fuck you, buddy. You're not the 'primary carer'. Of course not, you bastards. I fucking work so we can eat. I would like to stay home and watch my children grow, but I can't. We have to eat.

He is trying to reconcile me to the very likelihood that at this point, I have lost my children.

I haven't lost them. I didn't lose them. She stole them from me. Treacherous bitch.

Lunchtime

I'm in the car on my way to a rotary meeting, for which I'm already late. Today I'm on welcoming duty. I have to greet all members as they arrive. 'Hello. How are you going?' 'Welcome.' 'I'm well. How are you?' And so on to every member of the club. Can you imagine? I won't be able to handle it. I'm not a convincing liar. I'll pay a fine for being late so I don't have to talk to anyone. Hopefully, I'll disappear in a group.

Back in the office

Your friends desert you like you are a leper. They don't want to get involved. Quote, unquote. But if friends don't want to get involved, if that option is denied to you, the only avenues remaining are those horrific, bureaucratic, heartless institutions filled with rules, manned by the uncaring. Where someone makes a decision that will affect my life and the life of my family forever.

That's it.

Friends don't want to get involved. I think that's *crazy*. They are the only ones that can help. Friends and family. They are the only ones that can say to one, 'Look, you've got to try to do something.' We have no family here, so we have to rely on friends, and everyone wants to withdraw. To withdraw or to cut me out.

Or to take sides. Fine, take sides, but take sides in a positive way rather than 'Yes, I understand, and I'm sorry. I think it's not so good, but sorry, I can't help you, and I think I should stay out of it.' Fuck. Fuck you. A friend in need . . . I'm fucking in need, and they don't want to get involved. Who said? Who said that the best thing to do was to not get involved? Where is it written in concrete that says that when people are breaking up, friends don't get involved? What's the use of friends? What the fuck are they there for? Friendship to what end? To have fucking barbecues and get drunk with? What friendship is that? What about when you need them? They all think that not getting involved is the best thing to do. It's so wrong. Look, you bastards, if you can't/won't help, you cowards, keep out of this. Don't burden us with your opinions, and *don't take fucking sides.*

Why is there no one who wants to actively help? 'Of course, I want to get involved. I want to get involved.' I want someone to say, 'Yes, yes, *I want to get involved. How can I help save your marriage? Can I help you?' 'How can I help you *both*?' 'What can I do to help?' 'How can I help you mend things?' Not to help one against the other but help you repair because they understand that, in essence, that's best for everyone. They run for cover, thinking, 'Oh god, things must be so bad.' Be they as they may be, what can *you* do to help? *Cowards.*

———

I'm on a cycle of destruction. A cycle of destruction. And it feels as if I'm going against the grain. It all points in one direction, and that is destruction. Complete annihilation of my family. The process is finely geared towards concluding the destruction of my family as quickly and efficiently as possible. There is pain. I'm afraid of pain but more afraid of destruction. Give me the pain that repairs. Cut me, bleed me, and heal me.

Destruction rather than conciliation attempting repair. Mediation, conciliation, must be steps taken. Mandatory, if necessary, to save that which may be saved. Fuck the pain.

Just recently, my sister and her husband were having lots of problems. I was in contact with them. Marko, my brother-in-law, told me that things were not well in his view. My first reaction was to try to speak to my sister. I left a message. *She* didn't want to speak to me. What is this? Is this a woman's thing, to break away and burn bridges? She doesn't want to speak to me because she doesn't want me involved. What does that mean? Is this a woman's thing? I mean, what the fuck is that? My reaction was to go to Sydney to see if I could help. I was going to go to Sydney in April for my sister's birthday and also to try to convince my other sister that they needed counselling. To see if I could help in any way.

Sarah knew that. And she knew that I believed marriage was worth fighting for and saving. To give up on your marriage and to just let it go, without trying to save it, is wrong. She knows how important I believe marriage to be. My sister's marriage, let alone mine. She knows how important it is to *discuss* things. And she fucking walks out without talking.

I'm so confused.

If I knew where she was, if she'd told me she was going away and was going to be away for a period or God knows what, I would be angry and disappointed, but . . . but I'm just fucking confused. Confused that she would do this. That she would take my children. She's just run off with the kids. What have I done? I want to know what I have done to result in this nightmare.

A lot of people ask me if she has found someone else. I say no, she hasn't.

I don't believe so. I can't believe so. It will hurt me to the core. But if she has, it cannot hurt any more than this.

Have my homewreckers provided Sarah with another car as well so I can't recognise her? Are they so efficient at destruction?

If someone fronts at court claiming all sorts of things in the absence of the accused, the magistrate should *order* counselling. An order to attempt reconciliation. And if it fails . . . if that fails, then the court can do whatever is necessary. Hung and quartered. But to place a restraint on a man, keeping him away from his children on the hearsay of a woman, one person, is wrong.

Save my marriage, please! Please save my marriage.

Divorce is the natural conclusion. Divorce is always going to be the outcome. No wonder there are so many fucking divorces. This is not because there are so many sick marriages but rather because as soon as a marriage gets into trouble – as every fucking marriage must, at some stage, do – the whole process is geared towards destroying the marriage rather than trying to get it back on rail. There is no system that forces attempts at reconciliation. It is random luck. What fashion is this? What problem are we attempting to fix with this system of destruction? What is worse than the inevitable destruction of the family? 'Oh, my god, let's save this woman. Let's protect her. Let's cut her away from her horrible husband.' Gone. Finished! 'Next!'

McMarriage. 'Fries with that?'

Everything should point towards reconciliation between the parties, and only when that fails should other measures be brought into effect. But until that is tried, to do anything else is ludicrous. It is fucking *ludicrous*. The heartache, the human cost, the suffering of children, homeless children, single-parent families, social welfare, and crime. It is just outrageous. The cost to society, the debris of broken people resulting from an overemphasis on separation, is lunacy. Lunacy, a sickness of our time. A destructive overbalance. Destruction too readily available.

To prove that I'm not a child-molesting, wife-beating ogre or whatever else she has claimed to have a restraint on me, I'm going to have to get a report from 'experts'. These people are going to interview my children, or at least Claudia, to ascertain whether I have done whatever.

God, it hurts. Ahhh.

My eldest, my 7-year-old daughter. I have to rely on Claudia telling things without distortion. How will their questioning lead my child? I'm also concerned about the effect that the questioning itself will have on Claudia.

I smack my children. I say, 'If you do this, I'm going to smack you on the bottom.' Then if they do, I smack them once or twice – that's it, on their bottom – and then send them to their room. I'm not a beast, and I'm going to have to explain this in a credible way. I don't come across well. I've been in court a couple of times, and I'm very, very apprehensive because I've lost. In business, I've lost three times. I have been to court, and it smells of injustice.

My involvement in rotary is in question. It is very much a family-oriented organisation. I may no longer be part of a family. I don't belong. There are many reasons why I have been a member. One of the main reasons was that my children would benefit. When older, they could benefit through group exchanges, overseas exchange students, etc. If I'm not going to have my children with me, then why bother? Another redundant task to a single man.

There are many, many things that I do that are family orientated. They help to broaden my interaction with society. When the family is no longer there, then those issues lose significance. There are many things that I will have to do without, many things that I no longer need. I no longer need them because there is just me and no one else. No family. There's just me. I can survive with little.

There are certain freedoms, certain attractions to being alone. The advantages of being single. They are just an idea. They are not real. They are not really that attractive. They don't fulfil me sufficiently. I chose. I made the choice to be a family man, and I won't be satisfied otherwise. But the choice is no longer there. It has been taken from me. If I can't have the benefits of one, then I might, in time, indulge myself in bringing on the benefits of bachelorhood.

At home

It is now 6:00 p.m. on Wednesday. Day six.

No contact. Today I have received no calls from anyone. Everyone has vanished. No one is calling. Initially, people would ring because they realised it's serious and were showing concern. After a certain stage, they realised it's *too* serious, and they want to stay away from the pain. They fear the sight of carnage. So no one calls me. *Pain.* Not even Robin. Vautier was very supportive today. He knows I would never do the things that I may be alleged to have done and that I must prove I haven't done. He is Claudia's godfather and knows us well.

I walk around with a horrible knot in my stomach and indescribable sadness. I think of my children, and I still don't understand how she could take it so far. How she could do this.

I still hope that Jake is wrong. That this is not premeditated and that there is hope after this. I still hope there is.

I have to go through all this pain. Spiralling down a putrid tube with no exits.

TAPE 3

The Horror Continues

My children don't deserve this. They are good children, loving and innocent, with the joy of life. They are better off for me being around. I believe that. If I didn't believe that it would be a lot easier, I suppose. I do believe my children are better for me having been around and that they will be worse off without me. They will be worse off. I know. They're lovely kids. They're well behaved, caring, loving, and smart . . . and they love me.

I'm sure they love me. I'm sure they love me. If they know what love is, in their little way, 'cause they're so young . . . Ben is so young. His dependence on his mother is total. It has not been long since I was just a friendly stranger. Some stranger that he sees sometimes. Not often enough. I didn't wipe his little bottom. I wasn't there when he fell over and hurt himself, and I didn't see him take his first steps. As indeed, I didn't with any of my children. I wasn't around, so to some extent, I'm not essential. I'm important but not essential. But I still believe that they love me as much as they know how to love. I know that Claudia and Jessica do, very much. They are beginning to get a little maturity and wisdom. The test they are going to be put through – are they going to show that I'm not a horrible person that beats them up?

I'm sure that Sarah, when she began this, didn't expect this to go so far. This is what I believe now. I don't know. I'm just guessing – conjecture,

---

28

hypothesis. Trying to make sense of that which makes no sense. It may have been that she didn't expect it to last this long. But then I don't know why she hasn't made contact. This is really hard to understand. That she doesn't talk to me and leaves me in pain when she knows I'm in pain . . . not to even talk to me. I don't understand. I don't understand.

The other day when we finished the argument . . . the horror. The following day, I went into my stupid withdrawal mode. When I came home, she asked how I was, and I answered, 'I'm sad, lonely, and depressed,' which I was. I should have talked, said something. She wouldn't know that on that day, on that day, the finance broker refinancing some loans had called me to tell me he had run out of options. There were no options. He couldn't get it for me. That very day, the valuation upon which I was relying for another loan had come in far too low.

I've got Citibank on my back, McCavoy on my back. She wouldn't know that the day she served me with a restraining order was also the day that John rang me and told me that he was resigning. I can't understand how she could go away and not contact me.

Despite all, I love her. I love her, though she has caused me indescribable pain and has put our marriage on the verge of destruction. Whether or not it is destroyed, I don't know. I certainly hope not, but it may be. It is looking that way. Nevertheless, I love her. I just do.

And I love my children. I want my children back. I'm lonely. I'm lonely without them. I am not used to being alone. I haven't been away from them for longer than a day or so. I don't go interstate. My job doesn't call on me to go interstate. I don't go away from them for days at a time. I'm always with them. I always do things with them. I come home and make sure that I get home by six o'clock so I can have dinner with them. I like being with them for a few minutes in the morning. So little time. So little. I'm not used to being without my children.

I have to admit, I am sometimes short with them. I sometimes overdose on the noise because I'm not used to it. Maybe I could have handled that differently. I thought that they would always be around, so I just behaved in my then natural way. I wasn't constrained by the thought that they might not be around, confident that my marriage was sound. Now I think I would treat them differently, but that is affected by the fear and uncertainty that they may not be around. They are better for me being around. I'm a good father. I'm a good father. I know I am.

Where does this brutality come from? She's normally so kind. She's not at all cruel. I mean, I don't think she's cruel. She's hard-headed, and so am I. She's not perfect. But she's not cruel, and this . . . this is cruel. This is not like her . . . I don't know where she's getting this from. It's inconceivable to me that she doesn't even let me know what's happening. There is no contact. One minute there and the next, *gone*. If they were dead, I wouldn't suffer so much. No! That was a stupid statement, but I mean suddenly, it's all gone. I've lost my family. It's disappeared immediately, no fadeout. Poof! Gone!

I'm stupid enough to leave at work the sheet of paper on which I wrote the few phone numbers I've compiled. What a fucking idiot I am. I'm just not functioning. Every time I think of a new place where she might be, I think, 'Oh god, how stupid of me for not having thought of this before.' But each time, I've been wrong. Now I think she must be at a women's refuge. That too could be wrong. I have no way of knowing. Not knowing is killing me slowly. It's worse than death. At least in death, you know what happened. At least you know what happened. But this is *horrible*. I now understand the pain suffered by the family of those that are abducted. The pain of not knowing.

I can only imagine that Sarah is so sorry and ashamed that she cannot reverse the process she has put in place. A merry-go-round, triggered by her actions, from which she cannot get off. This is not a denial of my responsibility but rather acknowledging that the process has taken on a life of its own and we are both dragged along by its power. She may want to get off but can't. Maybe that's why she's not contacting me. Again, that's just a theory, another theory. Fucking theories with little evidence.

I'm talking a lot into this tape recorder. I think it is helping me. It gives me someone to talk to. I need to talk. And it won't judge me. A silent listener. At the back of my mind, there is always the hope that Sarah will one day listen to these tapes and the hope that she will then understand me. She would then realise that I would never, never, never consciously do anything to hurt her. I do not understand her. I harp on this lack of comprehension as to how she could do this without at least attempting to save our marriage. At least trying other means. This course of action is always possible but only after other avenues have failed. To do this to someone who loves you, to deny them their children . . . I . . . I don't understand it.

My father would be worried shitless as well. He wants us to be a happy family. He has also come to Perth to live with us. We were a stable family, and he intended to see the rest of his life out in the company of his son and his family. Now the whole thing has been put in question. We may not survive.

He must be thinking, 'What the fuck am I going to do in Perth if I don't have anybody here?' The other day, I told him that if things did not resolve, I would not be staying in Perth. This was more a reaction to pain. I don't know how far this is going to go, but I definitely want to see my children, and if I can only see them on the weekend, well . . . I mean, fuck, the whole idea of being part-time daddy is pretty hard to take. For *my* sake, I would stay. I don't think I could live without my children. I want them. I want them. I love them. They are my children, and I want to see them. When some of the pain has subsided and I get used to having them for . . . you know . . . whatever time. When all the pain is gone . . . if it ever goes . . . as it must do with time . . . I hope I'll stay to be with them.

How do they feel? What do they think is happening? What is she saying to them? What's she saying? What's she saying to them? That Daddy is a horrible person that can't be trusted, and therefore, they've gone away? How are they seeing this? What do they think is happening? Do they not ask, 'When is Daddy coming home?' 'Is Daddy coming home?' 'I want to play with Daddy.' Or do they not say anything and are quietly suffering? What are they thinking? How do they feel? Are they repressing feelings? I'm important to them too. They love me. How are they coping?

I have a card that I can leave on Sarah's car if I see it. The restraining order prevents me from going near her, so I cannot talk to her. Instead, I'll have to stick a message on her windscreen. I've got this card. I'm clutching at straws, of course. I wanted to be meaningful. I wanted something that would cause a breakthrough. The best that I could come up with are three questions:

1. Are you sure you know what you're doing?
2. Is this the best thing?
3. Who is it the best for?

This can't be the best thing. It just cannot be best. It cannot be best for my children. It can't be best for her or me.

I don't know what has got into Sarah's head, but I'm a good father. I think Sarah is a good mother. If I believe that she's a good mother, why doesn't she also believe that I'm a good father? Why are things so one-sided? Why does she judge me so harshly?

It's peculiar. I'm now hoping that Jake Carlino is right and I will be served with a notice of demand from a solicitor, her solicitor. Contact. At least then, I can start the process of . . . talking. For fuck's sake, at least it opens some line of communication. At last, some contact. Fuck, this is sick. I am hanging out to receive a fucking letter of demand from some bastard hired to do these things. What else can I hope for?

Eleven o'clock, Wednesday night

I've had no calls other than my call to Joan and a call from Tim Vautier. I rang Debbie, and she wanted to withdraw from the problem, and I left a message for Robin, which he hasn't returned, apparently also withdrawing. I feel like a leper. Everyone wants to withdraw – no one is prepared to help. I feel particular disappointment at Robin. He often tells me he loves me like a brother. What a lot of bullshit. He simply hums his 'feel good' message and does nothing. No one is diving in full bore. If enough people dived in and said that we should sort things out, we wouldn't be here. Wouldn't be where we are. I'm very disappointed with peer group withdrawals. What a bunch of gutless wonders I have as friends. They cannot stand to see the suffering, and rather than help me not suffer, they close their eyes and let me suffer alone.

The day when she served the restraining order on me seems such a long time ago. That was on Monday night. Today is Wednesday night, and it seems like such a long time ago. It seems like such a long time since she left me. It is just six days. Tomorrow will be the seventh.

God, fuck. Joan is trying. She's trying hard. She doesn't believe it's over and is prepared to do things to help me. Tim Vautier also is supportive. It's times like this that you establish whether or not the friendship was one of depth or a superficial one. It may be that with many people, it was too much to expect that our friendship would survive something like this. After all, what have we shared other than dinner a few times or whatever? Not prepared to . . . really help when I really need help. Who gives a fuck about having a few barbecues with people? Sociality. Friendship is help when someone is in trouble. I have very few friends. 'If there's anything I can do, please give me a call' – and they don't do anything. 'If you need to talk to anybody, call me' – and when you talk, they get embarrassed. The honesty/ severity of the problem embarrasses them. They get embarrassed by the proximity of pain. Or seeing someone else suffer and get embarrassed for them 'cause they are exposing themselves and they don't really want to know embarrasses them.

I dread the thought of the night. It is so long. I lie awake, fall sleep for a short time, and wake up again to stay awake for a long time. I stay awake for hours in the darkness with my thoughts. Dark thoughts. I hate it. I hate going to bed knowing I won't sleep. I masturbate to sap my energy, hoping to sleep. A daily ritual of self-abuse intended to numb me to sleep. It fails.

It's 4:02 a.m., and I've been awake for at least an hour. Just thinking. At this stage, my wish/objective would be that Sarah lift the restraining order on my children. Only on my children. And she can retain the restraining order on herself. Because otherwise, it will be three months before I get to see my children. By then, they may be strangers. Strangers to me. They won't recognise me.

I'm becoming resolved to seeing my children every so often, part time, whatever. I am becoming resolved to that idea. Also becoming resolved to the poss . . . the inevitability of us not reinstating the marriage. At this stage, I don't want a reinstatement of the marriage. I don't want her. I know we will have other arguments, and this has affected my confidence in dealing with Sarah. I would not be able to argue with her because she could do this to me again. I mean, what do I do next time? And we will have arguments again. There is no question about that.

I can't live under the threat of biased judgement. I can't live under those circumstances. It's unreal. It's unreal. I can't do that. I know I couldn't. I wouldn't. It's doomed.

I don't want Sarah back. I think she's a bastard. I think she's a bastard for doing this, and I don't want her back. I do . . . want to see the children. That means I don't want to see them in a month's time. I want to see them now. I want her to lift the restraining order. But she won't. She'll use it as a tactic against me. It's all tactics. This is unfair, unjust . . . It's not fair. She keeps the restraint on me to be as cruel as possible. Whilst she has a restraint on me, I see nothing but her cruelty and her attempts to hurt me. Which she has, deeply. I can't keep my mind on anything else. I really hope she turns back from this. I won't see my children for a month, but I don't want to see *her*. I don't want to see her. She's a bastard.

I have to burn the wound to stop the hurt. The hurt is unbelievable. Unspeakable cruelty. The pain that I feel is horrible. I want it to stop, have a break, rest and recover. And I know that I'm on a cycle of pain from which I cannot get off. I must ride it to the end. The end!

It is very difficult to operate at all under these circumstances.

I wish I could sleep.

Fuck, I'm tired.

I know this is leading nowhere. I cannot forgive her. And even if I could forgive her, how could I trust her? How could we be so far apart, me thinking that our marriage was sound and she killing it? I can't trust her. I have to resolve myself to the inevitability of divorcing. I don't want her. I don't want her. She's a traitor. I don't trust her. For the sake of the children . . . It is difficult. I don't want to hurt them . . . and I hurt. I believe if they grow up without a daddy, it will be wrong for them. And me.

I wake up in the mornings, run around, getting ready, have a cup of coffee, give them all little kisses, and race out. That's it. A very short interchange. At night, I get home and eat with them. Nothing much happens anyway. After dinner, they go to sleep. That's it. I don't see them much through the week. It's only on the weekend that I can spend some time with them. I enjoy being with them . . . I'm their father. But if, at the end of the day, this is what must be, then maybe seeing them a few hours on the weekends can be as good as I see them now anyway.

What crap.

I'm trying to rationalise to myself that which I don't want to believe . . . and I hurt.

I feel powerless. Absolutely powerless. My children are taken away from me. The State has jumped down my throat. I'm powerless to act.

It is going on to seven days now.

The whole scenario is too cruel. I just want to see my children, just to say hello! And kiss them and touch them. Smell them. Be near them. Ahhh. Make sure they are all right. See how they are perceiving events. If I can only see them every now and then, that has to be better than this.

Oh! I really should sleep.

I'm so tired.

At least I've found someone that will get involved. That will throw herself in to help. My sister Patricia called me and said she will do what she can. Call her family, whatever. She's on 'our' side. On the side of repair. I'm so grateful to her.

I've also thought of bringing Mary to Perth to testify on my behalf. As children, we fought. She used to beat me and scratch me, and I never hit back. 'You don't hit women. You're the boy. Protect your sisters.' The burdens of being the only son. Me, the protector of all around me – sisters, parents, family. I need her to prove that I'm not a wife beater, a child beater. This is ludicrous.

Day 7 — Thursday morning at home

I called Sarah's parents. I spoke to Rachel. Her hearing aid wasn't working very well, and I'm not sure how much she heard of what I was saying. They remember me for my 'horrific temper'. Albert's prejudice that all small men are aggressive . . .

I hope that she can pass on a message of reconciliation. I told her that the best thing she could do for us was to try to have our marriage mended. That I was prepared to do anything, that this is not the way to go. I'm not confident that I got through to them. There was an element of coldness there, of blame, of separation. As if I have already been shut out of their family. Immediate amputation. I could hear her father in the background saying, 'What has he done to her?'

'What has he done to her?' What have I done? What have *I* done? What have *you* done, you bastard? How have you poisoned your daughter, *all* your children? How has *your* desiccated marriage spoilt all chances for mine? Why am I paying your price? You dare to ask what I have done. You constipated piece of shit. *Cabron!* Me cago en tus padres!

In the office

This morning, at work, I rang Jake and the Family Court. I also rang the women's refuge to try to get a message to her. Not there. I rang the Lone Fathers Support Group and cried to them. I rang our doctor, and he is going to make an appointment for Monday to go see a psychotherapist. I'm fighting back. I did a lot of crying again this morning. Donna is very supportive. It must be peculiar to her to see her boss break down in front of her, but . . . I have. There is nothing I can do about that. I feel better now for having spoken to so many people and expressed my feelings to so many people. I need to do that.

I haven't much else to do. I can ring up the Samaritans at night if I need someone to talk to. Patricia is being very, very helpful. She's very clear and perceptive. Such issues as the hurt of Albert's accusations – 'What has he done to her?' – and what my children will think of me in time. She says these things are irrelevant. For the present, these issues are not important. She believes that what is important is how a man and a woman resolve their differences. I need to focus only on that. If it can be done. And on how to re-establish trust. That trust building will be difficult, if at all possible. It's good to have someone that seems to be rational, that can think. God knows I can't.

Whatever happens, I don't want her to ever, *ever* do this to me again.

I was entering the expressway to go to Leederville, and instead, I'm heading south on the freeway. It's just an indication that I don't know what the fuck I'm doing. Yesterday I hoed into some chicken, fried capsicum, and bread. I'm beginning to eat again, which is good.

The woman from the Lone Fathers Support Group to whom I had explained my circumstances consoled me by saying that it is very unlikely that the courts would rule against me seeing my children. The worst-case scenario has changed from one where I am not permitted to see my children for twelve months to one where I may not be seeing my children until April. After that, I should, in all probability, have access to them. She mentioned that I could apply for access through a Family Court solicitor without having to pay the additional cost. So at this stage, it looks like the worse outcome will be that Sarah and I don't get to see each other and that I have limited access to the children. A lot better than a couple of days ago. Also, whatever we own will be broken up. At least I will get to see my children . . . eventually. That is a great relief. That is a great relief.

Patricia was able to get me back on track about children loving unconditionally. Maybe that's true. Regardless of the poison being fed to them or the effect of this, I will, in time, regain their love. Priority number one is that I can love them.

I'm still optimistic of some form of contact so we can jump off this whirlpool of destruction. I can't believe that Sarah will hold out until April without contacting me. Jake is expecting a letter of demand from a solicitor. His experience in these matters makes him much more cynical. It's his job. I'm hoping that *she* will contact me and that she will lift these restraints on my children. Eventually, it must get through to her that I don't mean anybody any harm, let alone my children. I wouldn't hurt them, and she would know that. She *must* know that.

Where she is remains a puzzle. I believe that the best thing I can do is not to think too much. To go into damage control, pain control. Block out. Not think or feel too much. As much as possible, become numb so I can pass time more easily. Each day is so difficult. I do nothing else now other than think of this.

I spend time in the office, but I don't work. The business is being affected. Donna is in the office by herself now as I drive around aimlessly.

Business has been tough for many years. Recession, another unit that is empty, etc. The cash drain means that we're on our back foot. Costs are climbing. I'm spending a lot more. I've engaged a solicitor. Sarah would also be draining through her costs. I don't know if the business will bear it. When it comes to a division of property, I can't imagine how that's going to be done. I don't much care about that anyway. I don't mind closing up. This is the best excuse for giving up I can think of. My pride will not allow me to give up. I keep on fighting. But if my marriage breaks up, who could blame me for not being prepared to go any further? I don't know if we can anyway.

There are few people that can offer me any wisdom at the moment. In order of ranking, they would be Patricia, Joan, and Vautier. I'm very disappointed with Robin in that he hasn't done more. He has stayed away. It shows to me that our friendship was superficial, only good for barbecues, getting drunk, playing pétanque. Debbie has been more supportive than I would have thought, and I'm grateful for that. Giselle too. Jean has stayed away, but at least she was on both sides. God! You assess people in terms of whether they help you when in need, and I'm in need.

Today is the deadline of my message through Debbie that if she didn't contact me, I would call Jake. I doubt the wisdom of that threat, but it was my feeble attempt to get a breakthrough. If she feels at all like saving our marriage, I would hope for contact. It is after 1:00 p.m., and she hasn't contacted me.

At home

There is no letter at home.

I had a message from Vautier. Apparently, she has contacted Phillipa, and she thinks there is no chance of us getting back together.

I won't give up.

Apparently, she claims she has been trying to get me to do things for eighteen years. What thing? Possibly, I've been such a domineering character that I've pressed her too much.

In the car, driving in the vicinity of our house

I thought about getting an airplane that writes messages in the sky. I wanted it to write, 'SARAH, I LOVE YOU' in the skies over the northern suburbs, but I couldn't get one. Instead, I have made posters on A3 paper with the message 'SARAH, I LOVE YOU, PLEASE CALL ME' to stick up in all prominent places around North Perth, Mt Lawley, etc. Armed with these, I'm setting off. Every time I devise a new plan, I trill with excitement at the prospect that it might succeed. I won't give up on my marriage. I won't. I've got sticky tape, hammer, tacks, glue, and hope. I hope that it works!

Jesus! I don't know where to place these stupid things. Bus shelters, telegraph poles. I hope she sees them, and I hope that if she does see them, I really do hope that she will respond. I feel such a fool, sticking these things up. Everyone looks at me with the suspicion reserved for the insane. If I saw me through their eyes, I too would think of me as insane. There is no dignity in this chaos.

Back in the office

Yesterday's involvement by Clinsman wasn't very good. I guess they're like my father, who isn't being very helpful either. He is very anti-Sarah now as her family is very anti-me. I wish they would stop taking sides and be supportive of the marriage itself. Give support to the marriage itself and not to the individuals. I had to explain to them that I wasn't a . . . wife beater, excusing myself to my in-laws. They think I have a bad temper, which I do. Maybe they never liked me anyway and tolerated me for the sake of their daughter. In their minds, I must be guilty.

9:00 p.m. at home

I phoned Joy, Sarah's sister. She and I have been friends. She loves me too. I have explained the story so many times. I've said the same things so many times to so many people that I'm beginning to sound a little insincere. To me, I sound insincere, and I know I'm not. I can imagine that to those that are uncertain, I must sound completely ingenuous. I hope that Joy understands that I love her sister and that it would not be best for her, me, or the children to split up like this.

I was going to engage a private investigator to deliver a letter to her. Patricia convinced me not to take this step because if I did, Sarah would feel trapped, harassed, and she would probably bin the letter anyway. Even private investigators think I'm a ratbag when I tell them I have a restraining order. Strangers judge me. I may be dangerous. This also hurts.

I have to explain my position to so many people because I need help. If I didn't care, I would just give up. So what? But I do. I do care and do want to save my marriage. So I provide all sorts of private details to strangers. I don't want to tell anyone anything. I'm a private person. I prefer keeping things to myself. 'It's none of your *fucking business*. Get lost.' But that would only add weight to the contention that I *am* an irrational, violent person. I want them on my side, so I have to feign sincerity. It's so . . . oh god . . . It's despicable.

Day 8 — Friday, at home

Last time I saw my children was last Friday. I said goodbye to them before going to work. Sarah and Ben came into my office midmorning. She did something – I don't know, whatever she needed to do for business. Amazing. Little Ben was there with his little soft toy horse that screeches when pressed. I heard that sound coming from reception first and realised that he was there. When I saw him, I gave him lots of kisses, but he was bored in the office and wanted to leave as soon as possible. That's the last time I saw him.

I hurt. I'm no longer angry. I want release. I want to save if I can. I still believe that if I could talk to Sarah, I would be able to convince her that the best result for us is . . . Maybe I can't. But I love her. It is not for the sake of the children. It is for her sake, for my sake.

I'm resolved, day by day, of two things. First, that I won't give up, and second, that this is a long process, and I may not see her for a long time. I was away for two weeks in Sydney three years ago, and I missed her then. That was in a state of love. I'm going to have to get used to this, at least until she makes contact. Until I can convince her that we should not part. Until then, she needs time, whatever. I don't know, and it is going on and on. I've always thought that the longer it took, the worse it would become. I believe this. If I'd been able to grab it in the first couple of days and nip it in the bud, maybe . . . But that wasn't possible. Every day was urgent. Urgent to get to the problem quickly, put out the fire before it got out of hand. My world burns as I look on.

It has got out of hand. She has told people that it is irreconcilable, that she has had the same problems for eighteen years . . . Ahhh. That she doesn't want to keep the children from me, that it's only a temporary thing but that there is no chance for us. Ahhh! I can't believe that. I won't accept that. We have so much in common.

We were children when we met. She was 19, and I was 24. We have done so much together. So much together. She's so influenced by me, and I'm so influenced by her. I have made her, and she has made me. I can't believe that it can just end like this. It's not possible. I don't accept it.

———

How long is it going to take before she finishes with her roller coaster and comes to a plane? A plane where she is willing to talk? I know she would be going from anger to depression to sadness to frustration to vengeance and God knows what, but at some time as or when she is going through those emotions, she will get to a point where she's ready to talk. And I hope I don't blow it.

TAPE 4

First Contact/Solicitor's Letter

Friday midmorning at the office

Jake was right. He has received a phone call from a Peter Williams from a firm of solicitors acting on Sarah's behalf. He was told that she would be going to see them this afternoon at 1:30 p.m. When Jake told him that his client wanted reconciliation, that he loved his wife (I don't know how solicitors talk about these things), he responded that, in his opinion – and I'm not sure how he has arrived at his opinion, but in his opinion – that was very, very unlikely.

***

I went to the solicitor's building to paste up one of my posters. I'm not sure if she has seen any of the ones I've posted about the place. I asked to see the building's managing agent and waited in reception for his attendance. I wanted to ask his permission to put up one of my posters in the foyer. As I waited, self-doubt crept in, and I ran out of courage. I left the office without asking.

I've written a letter to her solicitor, and I've enclosed a letter to Sarah.

To Sarah's solicitor:

Dear Peter Williams,

Here is a letter to my wife. Please give it to her. I love my wife, and I don't want to part. I understand she is your client and you act for her. If it is irreconcilable, I understand your position, but please, let's not take any steps to worsen the situation unless all other avenues are explored.

I know this is unusual. I spoke to Jake Carlino, and he understands that, though unusual, I should try everything. I know you will try to do the best for my wife, but I hope that at this stage, the best is to try to work through our problems. Please, let's try those options first.

I would be very grateful if you could pass on this letter to Sarah. It is a very poor lifeline, but it is all I have at this stage.

Thank you.

And to Sarah:

Sarah,

I love you. First and last, I love *you*. I thought we had a good marriage. Not perfect but good. I was proud of us. I believed that any problem that we faced, we would overcome because we would face it together. I made the decision a long time ago that I would always love you. And I will. Please let me.

Whatever it is that is wrong, we will fix it. I hope that you still love me. I cannot think of life without you. Please make contact with me. Contact me in any way you want — by phone, alone, with others. I want to fix things between us. Please lift the restraint on seeing the children. You know I love them completely. I would not do anything to hurt them or to damage my relationship with them.

My heart aches without you, Sarah, my love. I have done nothing but think of ways of getting you back.

I have contacted anyone I can think of that may be able to help us get together. Don't give up on me, my love. Please don't give up on me. I know that we can work through our problems and that we will be better for having done so. Put aside blame, confusion, point scoring, hostility, and anything else that prevents you from helping us reinstate our family. The longer it goes, the more difficult it becomes to get back on course. Please don't allow the spiral of destruction to continue. Step back for my sake, for your sake, and for our children's sake.

Let's not become another statistic.

The restraining order hurt me deeply. Everywhere I went, I looked for your car. Clarkson, the Hills, Mosman Park, etc. etc. Every car engine I heard brought me to the front window to peek a look at you returning to our home. Every noise caused my heart to lift with hope that it would be you. I heard a noise at the front door and opened the door to two police officers who handed me a restraint order for you, for Claudia, for Jessica, and for Ben. They proceeded to explain, in their manner, what it meant. Making his point, the male officer pointed a finger at me and poked me lightly on the chest. He said that *that* would be a breach of the order, and I would have committed a crime for which I could be jailed. It was devastating. I would not do anything that would prejudice my chances of seeing my children. As much as it hurt me, I would not do anything stupid.

I had always hoped, believed, family matters were for and by the family. That they should sort their problems out without coercion from outside. Certainly, many times, the individuals involved may not, by themselves, be able to work through a problem, and so outside help is engaged in helping find a solution.

When I close the door at night, the world stays outside, and the family helps one another deal with whatever needs to be done. Or so I hoped. That night, the State kicked down my front door.

I have been through a roller coaster of emotions touching on helplessness, frustration, self-pity, powerlessness, alienation, love, compromise, remorse, surrender, self-doubt, fear, shame, humiliation, reconciliation, and many, many others. At the end of the day, the fundamentals remain unchanged. All else fades to insignificance:

- I love you.

- I love our children.

- I will do anything to keep our family together.

- Anything.

Please help me.

I have loved you for eighteen years. I hope to love you for fifty more years. Talk to me, please.

I cannot give up. I must not stop trying. I thought of hiring an airplane with a trailer message of 'SARAH, I LOVE YOU, PLEASE CALL' and having him fly up and down the northern suburbs. I couldn't get one, so I printed up some posters and put them up about the place. I hope you come across them.

Talk to me. Tell me what's wrong. Let's get help. Let's go to counselling together or separately.

I rang our doctor and got him to book me into a psychotherapist. I have been in contact with women's refuges, crisis centres, the Family Court, the Lone Fathers Support Group, and so on. I ache to the core.

The restraints can be lifted without blame or reprisals. If you don't want to see me, I won't. I won't come anywhere near you if you don't want (though I hope you do). I will not make matters worse. I love you. I love our children. Please, please let me see the children. They would be missing me. I know they love me. I hope they are asking for their daddy. You – who are there when they fall, who wiped their bottoms – have seen them take their first steps. I, who see them for a few moments a day and a few hours a weekend . . . I need them, and they need me. I will see them alone or with supervision or whatever you want, but please let me see Claudia, Jessica, and Ben. Let me kiss them and reassure them that I love them.

Let me talk with you. Let me woo you. If you want time alone, without the children, to talk, let's do that. Whatever you want, let's do it. But let's do it together. Let's do something, please. Sarah, please take a step back from the brink. Let's not fall into the abyss, where everyone loses. It is not the best solution for anyone. If, after trying every avenue, you still feel you don't love me or you'd prefer to part, then as hard as it will be for me to take that, I will have to accept it. But we haven't tried enough. We haven't tried everything to get back on track. We have to try. I feel strongly that it is too soon to call it quits.

We have been through a lot, you and I. We have had a lot of difficulties (many of them lately, including financial and business hardships). But we have also had many good times. Remember those, please. We were children when we met. We have matured together. We have so much in common, you and I. Please focus on that and not on the things over which we differ. You have been very good to and for me. You are a very supportive, loyal, loving person, and I am very proud to be your friend/husband.

Please, Sarah. I love you. I love your spunk. I love your moods. I love your body. I love your cheerfulness. I love your wisdom. I love your clear-sightedness. I love your support. I love your patience. I love your mothering. I love your eighteen years with me. I love your love. I love your toes, your bum, your eyes, your voice, your twat. I love your strength. I love your resolve. I love the children you have given us. There are so very many things I love about you. You must love things about me too. Please focus on those. Whatever the negatives are, let's work on them. I need your help. I need you now as I have always done.

Our children are better off for us both having been around, and I believe they will be better with us both remaining together. I'm not suggesting a compromise for their sakes because I would want you back if there were no children. But they are, and we are both very lucky to have them. They are beautiful children. They have a better chance of remaining that way if we sort out our differences. Please don't make me a weekend daddy. They need us. We owe them the effort in attempting to work through our problems.

You, Jessica, Claudia, and Ben are my all. Without you, nothing matters.

Because I love you so, I may have forgotten to tell you, simply expecting you to know. Sarah, my love, please talk to me. I'm going insane with worry and with not knowing. Call me, my love.

I love you, I love you, I love you, I love you, I love you, I love you.

So much depends on this letter, and I'm uncertain as to whether or not it's satisfactory. I don't know whether I've conveyed the fact that I loved her and, if I have, whether she'll believe me and, if she does, whether it will make any difference. It gives me a glimmer of hope. At least now we have some contact. Hopefully . . . hopefully . . . fuck, hopefully, she'll come back to me. I love her.

Why do these things become so inevitable once a certain step is taken? It picks up steam and churns along on its own accord. Why is it so inevitable that I will separate from my wife, whom I love and I'm sure, at the end of the day, loves me? Well! I may be wrong . . . She may not love me. She may have someone else. But I'm good for her . . . I think. She obviously doesn't think so. She doesn't think so now.

Is she a victim? Am I too domineering? What have I neglected to do? What should I have done for my marriage? What have I neglected to do that is so important that without it, she wants out? Does she have someone else?

God, I'm devastated. I need answers. I need understanding.

Afternoon at the office

I'll give Robert Howard a call today and resign from rotary, and I'll cancel my committee meeting for Monday.

Later in the office

I'm fighting off feelings of despair. Despair is not going to help me. I'm gagged. I'm bound. Chained. I can't move. I can't talk. I can't do anything. I'm so powerless. I'm firing off peas in the dark in the hope that one of them strikes home. Conjecture in a vacuum, little to go on.

Does this stem from economics? Is economics where the problem lies?

Does she feel that she's not getting a fair shake of the sauce bottle? Vautier mentioned that he hadn't seen her in a new dress in years. And it's true. We've denied ourselves luxuries for years. I thought tough times are to be shared. Are relationships so fragile? Do you have to give what you don't have because you are so insecure about the other person's love that you try to prop up that person's love? Does one need to buy love? I hope it is not over something as stupid as . . . No, I do! I do hope its finance. I hope it is to do with money. If it is over something as silly as money, then I can fix it straight away. One stroke of the pen, and the thing would be fixed. She can make all financial decisions. They're a bloody burden anyway. She can take over those roles. I don't own them. They are hers.

She's such a good woman. She's even good to my father. I just had an argument with him. Idiot! He's so fucking self-centred that even now he relates to everything from *his* perspective. He's so fucking stupid that he has an argument with me when I'm so *angry*. Doesn't he fucking know anything? I'm homicidal, and he argues with me. I'm so hurt, I'm tearing my hair out, and the idiot confronts me with his stupidity and selfishness. My whole being is in turmoil. My insides are bursting. Emotions are running riot. I could explode at any second, and he picks a fight with me. Idiot. At this stage, I could kill. Why is he drawing fire? The fucking idiot. Why draw fire? I'm dangerous, irrational. Stay away.

I am so ashamed. I am out of control. I threw my father out of the house and told him that he couldn't come in unless he tells me first. I know this is heartless, but I'm under siege. I don't want him to barge in using his key without me knowing. I don't want him or anyone else to find me in a state. The other day, I wrote a letter to Sarah. A very angry letter written a couple of days after she left me. I left it open on the kitchen table. It was intended for no one. I hadn't decided to send it to Sarah. He could have read it. These are private things. I just don't want him or anyone to see anything until I'm ready. I need privacy. I need to be able to act without having to maintain any pretence, to withdraw with my pain, to let it wash over me. I want to bleed in private if I have to and to bleed in public when I want to. I don't want encroachments. I'm in crisis, and I want to be me. I have no energy for pretence. I want to hide. I'm fragile, explosive, on 'senses overload'. I am unable to deal with my own pain, let alone those of others. I'm in my cave. Stay away.

Don't lean on me. I can't hold you. I'm falling. I'm falling.

Yet I am ashamed. My father loves me. He's on my side. He is helping as he can. But . . . I can't handle it. Not this too. No. Not this. I need *help*. My head hurts. It won't leave me alone. *Aaaaahhhhh!* I am sorry, Papa. I am not very strong. I am sorry. I am bursting.

I need to sleep. I need to rest. I need escape from my thoughts.

Day 8 — Saturday morning, in the car

I'm on my way to aikido.

Yesterday finished horribly.

My point of contact. My letter was useless. The response from her solicitor was that he'd given her the letter and she'd read it, and after that, she'd dictated her own letter. She dismissed my placing of posters in the neighbourhood as 'acts of aggression'. Her response was ten pages long, listing all the things she wanted, everything from the budgie to the camping equipment, lounge suite, two-seater. She wants everything.

Jake now asks whether now I can accept that the marriage is over. I'm tying him up. I'm tying his hands vis-à-vis this other solicitor. He wants to do what solicitors do and counter the other solicitor's attack. The letter said there was little chance of reconciliation and that this may well be final. Having read her letter, I have to come to the conclusion that it probably is.

The dilemma is that I still want to reconcile, and I don't want to do anything that will prejudice the chances of doing so. Yet at the same time, there have been so many attacks. So many steps taking us further and further apart. The time may have come for me to attempt to protect myself. To return fire.

Do I have to? Is this best?

Jake claims this letter is a tactical move. I received it 4:30 p.m. on Friday to offer me as little time as possible to respond. He has given me until Monday to consider my position and has told me that we must respond. Otherwise, they will petition the Family Court claiming I'm a bastard – that I'm not looking after the children's welfare, that I'm under restraint – and get a court order to enforce whatever they want.

I don't know which way to move. The stakes are too high, and I can't afford to make mistakes. I don't want to get into a fight over trivial things. Whether she owns a record, a plant, or a ring. Whatever. Also, I don't want to see the house destroyed, dismantled, yet. I don't agree that it has to be done. It's only been seven days. It's such a speedy annihilation of eighteen years. One-day destruction for every thousand days of living together. Surely, this isn't inevitable. It can't be.

My children. I don't want to make it irreversible for them through a process of arguing over petty things. She has listed business and property, everything. After we argue about that, all will be lost. No chance after that.

Do I allow myself to be raped in the hope that eventually, she'll come around? Do I, for self-preservation, contest and fight back and, in doing so, increase hostilities? It's too difficult a decision. I don't know which way to go.

I rang her mother again. Why did I bother? I'm such a slow learner. Her view is 'She's left you. It must be your fault. You have to look at yourself. What have you done to cause her to do this?' Such narrowness, lack of wisdom. There is no balance. It's such a shame that they are not helping with reconciliation. To support her in her actions towards saving rather than destroying. So one-sided. Such small-minded destruction from people who should know better. At the end of the day, in six months' time, in a year's time, in two years' time, I know she will realise this is a mistake. But it will be too late. She will die knowing that when her daughter really needed her wisdom, she erred. She was too stupid to make the right decision.

This cannot be the best thing to do. Not yet anyway. She's not thinking of the children. I love her for her, not the children, but she's not thinking of the children. Jake says that if she is as hostile as she appears to be in the 'access to children' issue, I may only see my children every second weekend. They're going to grow up without one parent. It can't be. It can't be good for them, for her.

It's not good for her. She has three children. It's hard. It's hard living alone with three children. What is she thinking? Is life with me so horrible that she prefers the hardships of single motherhood to being with me? I can't understand it. Why doesn't she talk? I'm so confused. I blame myself, of course, but is life with me so bad?

At the dojo

I'm at aikido. There are a few people here. I've given the guys instructions, and I'm training alone. Going through the movements. I hope to lose myself in kata.

Sunday afternoon

Self-preservation is kicking in. I'm ironing some shirts for the week. Today . . . I don't know about tomorrow, but today I'm beginning to accept that the marriage is over and that there is nothing I can do about it. One week on, and our relationship of eighteen years has vanished.

I wrote a letter and took it to Belinda. I was hoping that she could give it to Sarah, but she said she didn't want to get involved. She wouldn't even take it. Most people's marriages are not that secure. They feel it might put their marriage in question. That's what Michael Court said anyway, which is quite wise, I suppose.

Claudia called this morning, and I just cried. I bellowed like a bull. It came unexpectedly, out of the blue. I cried and told her that I loved her and her brother and sister. She said she loved me too, and that was it. She said that Mummy would not come to the phone. I could have said so much to her, my little darling. I could have also spoken to Jessica and Ben. I could have tried to find out what is going through their minds, if they are well. I could have spoken to all of them. I could've but didn't. Instead, I wasted the opportunity by my yearning to speak to Sarah. Wasted my time with lovely Claudia pitifully yearning for answers from Sarah. I don't know when they'll ring again. So many mistakes. I make too many mistakes. What will this mistake cost me? When will I next get to speak to my Claudia, my Jessica, Ben? Will this be another stick to beat myself up with if contact is long in the distance?

I've gone through the list that she provided me and have conceded most things. They're useless fucking things anyway, full of painful memories. I'm better off without them. There are certain things I won't give her but not many. I also want her to move back into the house, and I will move out. At least then, the children can be in the family home. I am prepared to pay all costs for her to do so. Preservation is slowly working its way in. I'm feeling better about her action, her cruelty. On top of sadness is resentment. It was a horrible act.

Patricia – who has, until now, been attempting to reconcile our relationship – is coming to the opinion that Jake is right, that the marriage is over and I should retrieve whatever is possible. From her perspective, Sarah has left the home so she can fend for herself. I don't want to do anything that is going to make my children's lot any more difficult than it needs to be, but the business cannot afford to conduct a protracted legal action and sustain two households. It's in an environment of deteriorated performance because of me not giving a fuck.

She can move back, and I move out, taking the few things I need. If she doesn't want to move back in, I'll let her have whatever she wants from the place. Even if she doesn't want to return, I'll have to quit this house. I can't live here. This is our family home, the home where my children lived. This is not my home. I cannot live here alone.

It hurts. But it's turning from blind hurt to blame hurt. 'I'm hurt, and it's her fault that I'm hurt.' I'm hurt because she has been cruel to me. I'm hurt. She stabbed me in the back without warning. I'm hurt. She has stolen my children. I'm hurt because she placed a restraining order on me. I'm hurt because of the speed with which she is dismantling our house, our marriage. I'm hurt because she won't talk to me. I'm hurt because she viewed my expression of love in the posters I put up as an *act of aggression.*

I'm hurt because she has destroyed me. I'm hurt, and I blame her. *It's her fault that I hurt.*

Whatever it is that I have done does not deserve this. I still don't know where she lives. Such . . . such cruelty. Such premeditated cruelty.

My life rots like the fruit in the fridge. Who gives a shit about fibre?

Monday

I've written to Jake with my response after discussing it with Mary. I have called for cohabitation. I didn't think it would be acceptable, but Mary convinced me that I should at least try. Sarah's solicitor thinks that this is out of the question, but I've insisted that it be put to her. I want *her* answers, not his. I doubt that this course of action will provide us with a solution, but it's worth trying.

I need to hate. I need to hate to deal with the pain. The pain of losing my family. The pain of treachery. I need to hate. Hate is less debilitating than pity. I need hate to purge the pain. The pain of silence, not knowing where she is. I need to hate to deal with these solicitors who are going to destroy our family. I need to hate. I don't know how to hurt her without hurting the children. I don't know how to get a clear shot at her. Whilst she hides behind those I love most, I can't get at her. She's a pig, a cowardly pig.

I slept reasonably well last night. I was OK late afternoon yesterday, a little more peaceful. This morning too, the clouds of doom dispersed slightly and temporarily.

I resigned from rotary.

It is 2:30 p.m. The clouds have returned. I have closed the door to my office, and I'm crying alone. So far, Donna is the only person in the office that is privy to my turmoil. Am I destined to be alone? Will old age find me alone? Why won't she talk to me?

It is 7:30 p.m. I'm home alone, watching television. 'Current affairs' this week has centred on family issues. It is the 'international year of the family', and my family is dissolving. My family will not have an international year. Advertisement is full of *happy* families. All movies are about love and that sort of stuff. I can't handle it. I tried to sleep but couldn't, and now I'm sitting here, wondering what the hell to do. I don't want to ring people and bother them with *my* problems. I've done enough of that. I don't know if I can sit through a whole movie or video. I don't want to go to a bar. It's too lonely. I don't know how to just hang out at a bar. I feel as if my problems are written all over my face. I don't know what to do to fill in time. It's only 7:30 p.m. I have hours of waking time before I can try to sleep. Hours. So much empty, purposeless time.

She too would be suffering. She must be. I don't understand how she could be so cruel to me. How she could . . . she could go on so long. She could break off hostilities at any time, but I don't know how. All she'd need to do is to make a bloody phone call, and things would change. She has the power to change the course of our lives. She's so stubborn. She's so strong. Heartless. I still don't know what I've done.

Tuesday, 8:00 a.m.

I'm in my car, ready to go to work. I feel a little strength. Resigned and sad. I wonder what horrors today will bring. Jessica *always* used to wave to me from my bedroom window as I drove away to work. Sometimes Ben and Claudia also waved. There's no one waving me goodbye today. The window is empty.

It is raining. I would take Claudia to school on days like these. I drive away alone.

It is 9:30 a.m. I went to a dentist's appointment today at 9:00 a.m. It's for next month. I was one month early for my appointment. I am lucky to have thought of it at all, let alone remembering the right time.

I'm trying to take the initiative and tie things up to slow down the process so we do what is best rather than act in response to the life this process of destruction has taken. Instead of responding to her attacks, I am making my own suggestions to which she needs to respond. I can guess her response, but I try nonetheless.

I am fighting a rear-guard action for the sake of my marriage.

Even though the clouds are thin, my stomach is a mess. Tight. I wonder if hers is also tight.

We had a bit of a breakthrough today. It seems as if she is prepared to allow me to see the children from Saturday afternoon to Sunday afternoon. She has decreased hostilities to some extent. She may be taking her foot off the accelerator of destruction. We need time, a little time. We don't have to destroy everything in a hurry.

I saw her car up on a hoist at her petrol station. She is obviously in the area. I still love Sarah. She's such a good woman. I hope she hasn't found someone else, that there is still hope that I get an opportunity to prove to her that I love her and that I will do as much as is required to get our love back on the rails. She's such a superwoman.

I changed the locks at home today. It's a defensive measure, and I don't know if it was such a good idea. I feel so insecure. She can go there at any time whilst I'm at work and do whatever she pleases. She has all cards stacked her way. I'll change them back as soon as we get some resolution.

If she lifts the restraining order on the children, I would be very happy. I'm resolved to the likelihood of termination anyway. Seeing the kids is paramount. Anything else would be a bonus . . . but I do want bonuses. I crave bonuses. I love her. I hope this is all the result of anger and frustration and that when she cools down, she'll realise that she loves me and that she prefers life with me to life without me. I love her very much.

I'm very disappointed with her parents' behaviour. I am mainly disappointed at their lack of wisdom and their immediate hostility towards me. Why don't they help? I thought we were family and that they would side with attempts to bring us together. Fools. They could have helped put a stop to this earlier or even now. Help to not make it so destructive, so terminal. They didn't, and I'm extremely disappointed. My sisters have been very good. Instead of taking sides, they've been trying to build bridges for us. They know that what is best for me is to repair my family. They are helping in a constructive way. They help me by helping us. They have contacted Sarah's parents. No one from her family has contacted my family or me. Such small-mindedness. Such jellyfish. Such constipation.

I'm glad I took the initiative to making proposals to Sarah to show that I'm concerned about the children. I love her anyway. Despite all, I still love her, and I do not want to hurt her.

I dropped off another letter to her solicitor. I don't know if she has read it yet. I hope she reads it in the way that I had intended. My last attempt was such a failure. I want her to know that I don't want to make an enemy out of her. If she is never to love me again, I don't want her to be indifferent to me. I want her to remember the good times. If she can't live with me, for whatever reason, she should remember we have spent half of our lives together. I don't want her to feel bitter and twisted about our relationship.

Sarah,

For our children's sake, break off hostilities. Let's not deal through solicitors. We have both already experienced the disbenefits of that.

I want to see my children. Please don't stay on this course.

If reconciliation is impossible, so be it. I am attempting to control my feelings of hostility towards you for the sake of the children. No doubt this will help me to, in time, fall out of love with you. Nevertheless, break off hostilities so that the anger on both sides subsides enough for us to decide what is best for us individually and for our children. Let time clear the clouds of anger and hatred to see clearly what is best. Let us not look back on this in six months, twelve months, or whenever and feel sorrow for having conducted our termination in a poor way. Let us not regret our actions in the future.

What will be must be, and we will all have to accept it, but don't keep pushing towards destruction without time.

Regardless of how long you have been planning this, you have done so in a vacuum. This is now real. Don't let yourself be carried by the course of events. You are the boss. You can stop things. Give us time to think of alternatives.

Seeing the children is paramount. Please consider how you would feel if the reverse were the case. I love them more than anything. For their sake, I'm trying to prevent me from taking retaliatory actions. Think what you would feel if, without warning, I had acted as you have. I need to see them.

Let us be humane, even in our anger, for the sake of all the beautiful memories that we must both have of our eighteen years together.

This letter is probably, again, inadequate. I'm firing off shots in the dark. Don't take it for anything other than what it is. Remember me. You know me. This letter is for us.

I understand that this may be final but let's act as people who have shared half their lives together, who love or have loved one another.

Be guided by your decency and heart, not by anger and hatred. No one but you knows me or I you. Take counsel of your soul, not from people who have no interest in the welfare of our family.

If this letter is, again, off target, write or phone or whatever to me and let me know why, but let it be you, not some hired destroyer of families.

—

Please, Sarah. Don't do this.

I'm eating again. The spin-off benefit of slimming down will soon fade.

This house is horrible for me. I can't stand it. It's so empty and lonely. I'd be lonely anywhere, but this place has too many memories. I have to move out. Each room is crowded with the ghosts of the past, the decaying stench of memories. I have closed the doors to all rooms except my room, the kitchen, and the bathroom. I don't want to see the emptiness, childless children's rooms, and loveless lounge room. I'm trying to obliterate the vision of emptiness, which burns my soul. At the same time, I think that the kids would prefer to visit me here. My remaining in this house is probably best from the point of view of our children. When they visit me, they will be 'coming back home' instead of visiting me in some strange house. I will have to stay here, at least for the short term. Staying here will be very difficult, but I am destined to it so I can reconnect with my children.

Also, if she returns with the children and I move out, it would be more normal for the children. If she doesn't, I would benefit in rebuilding my relationship with my children by living in the family home.

I know I make mistakes. Mistakes at the moment can be devastating. But I've got to do what I feel to be best at the time and hope it is the right decision.

I'm drinking lots of water and very little coffee at night, but I still can't sleep.

Day 13 — Wednesday

I'm back home from work. I'm trying to make sense of things at work. I've had to pick up the threads of Sarah's work. Taking up her role in our business mid-flight is difficult. I have been trying to thread together the pieces to ensure that our service to clients does not suffer. They need not know. It is not their problem. I'll cope.

Taroo cries. She's alone all day when she's used to having the company of Sarah and the kids. I'm often not here even at night, and when I am, I am not great company. She echoes my feelings with her painful howls. Taroo, wise, loyal, beautiful, playful companion to my children and me. Poor Taroo. She has been such a good friend to us all. Now she too is alone.

Thursday, end of Day 14

Still at work. I'd like to go out and do something with someone. Go to the Festival club or some such. I still haven't heard from Jake to see if an agreement has been finalised. I don't know whether I'm going to see the children this weekend or not. I'm lonely and bored, but I'm getting better. The clouds are thinner today.

Day 15 — Friday

Last night, I went to the Festival of Perth nightclub. Donna convinced me that I needed to get out and have a little fun. I called a few people and arranged to meet them there. Donna picked me up after dinner. I was the passenger.

We were the first to arrive. Donna and I chatted a little self-consciously. The arrival of friends didn't help to ease my discomfort.

Introductions.

'Where do you know each other from?'

I felt as if I was living a stereotype. 'Lonely boss seduces/is seduced by his secretary'.

We drank on.

As the night wore on, more acquaintances arrived. Sensitive issues were avoided, but there was obvious surprise that Sarah and I were no more and that I was with another woman. None had known me as a single man. My intimacy with Donna was apparent for all to see. Also with us was Anne, who has been living in London for some two years. We chatted about trivialities and drank some more. She ignored Donna.

Alcohol released me. I had been my mind's prisoner for too long. The chains were eased, and I was pleased to be allowed not to think. Clouds diluted, alcoholic peace.

Donna was beautiful. She stayed near me, joining in whenever she could, uncomfortable at not knowing anyone, and the object of subtle hostility by those that would not accept me as anything other than half of a couple. By the time we left, I was quite drunk. She drove me home. We were both laughing at nothing, having had a good time.

When we arrived, she got out of the car and walked me to the front door. I fumbled for the keys, opened the front door, and turned to Donna, and we locked arms in passion. I immediately began to grope her, fondling her breast, rubbing her crotch as we devoured each other.

'Come in. Stay.'

'No, we shouldn't. I've got to go. It's late. We have to work tomorrow.'

'No, don't go. Stay. I want you to stay.'

I cupped her buttocks with my hands and walked backward as we kissed. As soon as we were inside, I closed the door.

We kissed as I felt her skin inside her clothes. I clumsily unbuttoned, unzipped, undressed her. We were partly dressed as I led her to my bedroom, taking little notice of the emptiness. Once there, we fell on the bed.

I was horny as hell, being used to frequent sex with Sarah. I had not been with a woman for what seemed like an eternity.

My sex with Donna was urgent, desperate. I struggled with the condom packet, trembled as I slid one on. Once inside, Sarah invaded me.

'Inopportune bastard. Leave me alone. What are you doing here?' Thoughts of Sarah, my children, separation, and restraining orders invaded my present. My mind was a potpourri of guilt, lust, hunger, embarrassment, loneliness, doubts, and sadness, all awash in alcohol. At the same time, my cock lacked sensitivity. The alcohol and my unfamiliarity with condom sex were combining to emphasise the effort required to fuck. Running a marathon, I was breathless. I struggled to drive Sarah from my mind, and I hurried on.

'God, this feels good. She's beautiful.'

'I wonder where my darlings are. Why has she done this?'

'No, no! Concentrate. You need this. She's fucking gorgeous.'

'Where am I going with this?'

'I can't do this. I should stop. How?'

'No, keep going. You have to finish.'

'You're nearly there. *Keep going.*'

Finally, I came. Release. Relief. Guilt.

I'm certain that Donna too was relieved.

We basked in each other's embarrassment as we panted to repose. As the aggression of lust faded, tenderness returned. Gentle touching re-established our intimacy. I felt privileged by Donna's affection and support. The gleam of perspiration on her skin made her even more beautiful. As we lay in each other's arms, I breathed in the smell of our sex.

Then the torment returned. My mind darted from the enjoyment of the pleasures of the moment to the guilt of betrayal and the grief of loss. At the same time, I was aware that the stakes had been raised. Another person had moved from a peripheral position to centre stage, and centre stage was already too crowded. What would my relationship with Donna be if

I were successful in reconciling with Sarah? This must surely up the ante in Sarah's mind if she were to find out or if she were to care sufficiently. I also felt ashamed at my weakness at having succumbed to the obvious. My body's mind had ruled but only momentarily. Upon fulfilment of its objective, it had retreated, abandoning me to face the scorn of my guilt on my own. It was relentless, darting from one painful thought to another.

Donna's touch was soothing. She didn't stay long.

The night was torn.

Today I'm hung-over. Donna and I avoided each other this morning, feeling a mix of guilt and embarrassment. By lunchtime, we were talking about the night before and what fun we'd both had, though avoiding references to sex.

The relief that alcohol and sex provided me has allowed me to resolve a couple of things. I've agreed to her taking whatever she wants. She is insisting that Robin represent me whilst my home is being emptied and that I'm to be away. I won't agree. I want to be present at the rape of my home. She can have anyone she likes represent her. She won't come, but I'm going to be there. I need to see it dismantled piece by piece. I believe that is better than leaving a full house and returning to an empty shell. I know what that feels like and don't want a repeat.

Home after work

She agreed.

Tonight, is the last night I will spend in my house before it is dismantled. I'm howling with pain. I walk from room to room, breathing in the memories that live in these rooms, beds, clothes, etc. I walked into Ben's room and buried my head in his bedclothes. I inhaled his scent. Wiping my tears with his clothes, kissing them.

Agony.

I'm losing my mind. This is crazy. I'm going crazy. The neighbours must think a lunatic lives next door. I've bellowed uncontrollably, thrown myself against walls, hoping to find release from my torture in physical pain. I head-butted the wall. Hard. It hurts. But my thoughts follow me everywhere. I can't escape.

I'm dripping wet. I've splashed water on my face, my head, my chest. Crying is hot. My face is red. I'm burning. Despair comes in waves of uncontrollable sadness, anger. Then it subsides, momentarily. It returns in burning fury. I studied my face in the bathroom mirror, pitying the wretched creature looking back at me. I am unrecognisable. My face is distorted with pain, red hot from crying. I watched the water/tears run down my face, chest. Splashing water on me offers me physical relief. The floor, carpet is wet.

The water doesn't cool my brain. There is no escaping my mind. It will not leave me alone. Memories, regrets, doubts, anger, grief, loneliness torture me . . . without reprieve. I wish I could tear out my brain. I wish I were somewhere else. My mind was somewhere else. Or dead. I wish I could get off this roller coaster of pain. 'Stop this. I want to get off.' I can't handle it. It's too much. 'Don't . . . don't. Go away, head.'

I am a coward. I would like to die. The best of life is gone. But I can't do anything to prevent it. Powerless. I feel trapped by my obligations to my children. I don't want them to grow up without a father. I don't want Sarah or anyone to believe I have done it *against* them. I don't want my life on *their* conscience.

But I don't want to be here. I don't want to live.

Economically, my children would be better off if I were dead. I'm well insured.

My father just phoned. He has invited me over to eat with him. I'm going to see him. I need to get out of here. I'm fucked.

Saturday morning

Another sleepless night. I'm preparing, waiting for the rape of my home. She's sending people over with removalists to finalise the physical destruction of my home.

Last night, I walked over to my father's house. As soon as I saw him, I began crying.

He cried with me, saying, 'No te preocupes, hijo. Esto pasara.'

I have not cried in front of my father since before my teens. I was a child again, and he comforted me. I love the man. He has done so much for us, provided me with an example I will not be able to imitate. 'Padre, te necesito.' But I was not able to tell him how much he means to me. He made me a small steak. I ate half of it. As I left, I noticed how much he was suffering for me. We have become good friends, my father and I. He is my only family in Perth, and I've leaned on him a lot recently. He often bears the brunt of my pain. He supports with few demands. I love him and wish him not to suffer for me. I'd like to shield him from my suffering, but I don't have the strength. I'm sorry, Papa. 'Lo siento, Padre. Perdoname. Me duele mucho. Perdoname, Papa. Perdoname.'

On Tuesday or Wednesday of last week, she proposed that I could get to see the children if I agreed to her having sole custody. This, she negotiated whilst I am squeezed by the restraining order. Heartless tactics. I had to agree. I want to see my children. She has not yet lifted the restraining order. Jake advises against me seeing the children until the order is lifted. He smells a set-up. She's being an absolute cunt.

Belinda and Rachel represented Sarah. Rachel has flown in from Noosa. They had their copy of the list, and I had mine. We went from room to room, emptying them in an orderly fashion. Robin was with me. He helped to 'lighten' the mood, cracked a few jokes. The removalists were quiet and solemn. They told Robin it was the worst job they'd had to do.

As the rapists left, Belinda bid me farewell with the words 'Look after yourself'. Look after myself? Look after *myself*? I have been looking after the welfare of five people for years. Looking after myself is a breeze. Look after myself. 'Look after yourself, you fat turd.' She obviously knew where Sarah was staying and probably knew all along. Her 'not wanting to get involved' was a sham, a deceitful sham. I will never forgive her. I will never forgive the part she played in the destruction of my family. The lying cow will be an enemy for life. I will never, *never* forgive her.

Last night I wrote . . . a . . . little letter . . . to my children. I hope she lets them read it. I wrote that I love them and not to forget me. I gave it to Sarah's plundering cohorts.

My lovely children, Claudia, Jessica, and Ben,

Tomorrow people will come and take things away from our family home into a new place. I hope it is a nice place and that you are very comfortable and happy there.

You probably don't understand what is happening. To tell you the truth, neither does your daddy. But whatever happens and no matter what people tell you, please remember, always, that your daddy loves each of you very much. You are my children, and I will always love you. I'm very sorry that I can't see you yet. I would very much like to, but I am not allowed to see you.

I miss you all very much, and I'm hoping to be able to see you very soon.

Taroo and Yayi also miss you lots and lots, but we will all be very strong, and this time will pass very quickly.

Please don't forget me because I would be very sad if you forgot all the good things that we have done together. Or how much you mean to me.

Remember, I will always be here if you need me for anything at all. As you get older, I will try my best to be the daddy that you need. Even if we don't see each other for long times, don't be shy with me. I am your daddy, and you have nothing to be embarrassed about with me. You are my flesh and blood. You are of me. You are me.

Claudia, you are the eldest, and so you will remember me the best. Please look after your brother and sister and don't argue too much with Jessica, as she shouldn't with you. Jessica, you, as the middle one, have to make sure that you all help one another. Ben, be nice to your sisters and learn to be a big boy soon.

There is so much I would have liked to share with you all, my beautiful children. I wanted to be around more and to see you grow up, but life has many turns, and this is now impossible.

I love each and every one of you more than anything in the whole world. Remember me and remember all the good things we did.

I will always be around for you.

Your Daddy

Robin stayed with me in my empty house and tried to console me. We talked until darkness. I prefer darkness.

Monday night

I've just been out with Roy. He invited my father and me to watch a game of soccer.

This morning, I went to my psycho for counselling. I don't believe there is much chance of reconciliation. I don't know if she will lift the restraining order. The hearing date is only ten days away. It's been a long time since she did this bastard thing. I'm alone, lonely, and trying to pick up the broken pieces of my life. I feel sorry for the kids. They will suffer, but it is beyond my control to do anything. I'm trying to fall out of love with her. She doesn't deserve my love. And she doesn't love me. No call. I still don't know where she lives. Still no contact with my children. Still no lifting of the restraining order.

Her mother went through my place like Epsom salts and took everything, including the old lock to this house. She used to call me her 'favourite son-in-law'. Ignorant hypocrite.

The division of property has begun. I faxed to Jake to let him know that I wanted a resolution of property settlements. This and access are the two outstanding issues.

I feel sorry for her. I feel sorry because when she wakes up from her present nightmare, she will regret her actions. She must, in time, realise that what she has done is wrong. It's becoming very late. I can't see her agreeing to *my* demands. (Ha! 'Demands'.) I can't see her doing the things *she* would need to do before *I* would have her back. She has been too cruel. Even my shrink can't believe it, and he's seen lots of these types of cases. I told him the whole story, including the night we argued.

It's such a pity. I feel sorry for her with three kids, 37 years old, alone. I'd like to see the children today, tomorrow, the day after . . . as soon as possible. But she won't let me. She's being an absolute cunt about this. That alone is unforgivable.

I'm beginning to think of other women. I'm horny as hell. I'm socialising 'on the make'. I said to Robin the other day that if I was falling back onto the 'meat market', I was coming back as a rooster, not a pig. Today I ate a little more than normal, but most days, I eat lots less than I used to, and I'm losing a lot of weight. I'm doing my 5BX exercises and feel neat and trim, physically strong.

I joined Dinner for Six as a way of meeting people. Three males and three females, strangers, go out to dinner and talk about whatever. Neil Costa recommended it to me. That's how he met Joy. Fuck you, Sarah! It's like an introduction service. I don't want a replacement at the moment, but I need company and things to do to fill in my days. I can't rely on the few friends I have. It isn't enough. My circumstances are different. My needs are different. They belong to a previous life. In a previous life, they were my friends.

I always felt that when people have different jobs and different interests, they can grow apart. I was pleased that Sarah was involved in our business. But we grew apart anyway, right under my nose. We grew apart without me even noticing. The whole thing is incomprehensible, even from an intellectual point of view. Emotionally, it is hurtful. How does something like this happen? How does it happen?

Tuesday

I'm off to work now. I stopped at the top of the driveway where Jessica always used to wave to me. There's no one waving now, of course, except in my memory. Jessica, lovely Jessica. I know you would prefer to be with your daddy. Jessica, my love, like me, second-born, a beautiful child.

Thursday

The process grinds away without resolution. I still have not seen the children. The order still applies. Sarah and I stifle on through solicitors.

My father has been a great help. He is very supportive. Whilst I'm at work, he comes over and waters the garden and tidies up around the outside of the house. He has kept the garden alive. Most nights, he tempts me with an offer of dinner at his place. We talk about soccer and other things, anything, so we do not touch on a subject that causes us *both* a great deal of pain. He asks, 'Algo nuevo?' and when I reply, 'No, nada,' we change the subject. We each avoid discussing the monster that lurks above us, looking on, for fear it will devour us. Sarah took the washer. I drop off my washing to him, and he returns my clothes to me clean. I'm a child again, and he, my father, is protecting me, looking after me. Te quiero mucho, Padre. Gracias.

Saturday

No development. For quite some time now, there appeared to be some agreement in place for me to see the children. This bastard. 'Agreement'. A 'Section 66ZC agreement', they call it. Whilst she held a gun to my head, she insisted on sole custody and reduced my access to my children to Saturday, 5:30 p.m., to Sunday, 4:00 p.m. An 'agreement' I could not refuse. Whilst unpalatable to me, I've had to agree. I'm desperate to see my children. She holds them and the restraining order as aces to use against me. The children are pawns in her manoeuvres against me. The bitch.

There is yet no agreement to seeing my children. She claims that she's open to 'amending' the restraining orders, but she won't lift them. 'Amending'. What amendments, you bitch? You have no right to keep my children from seeing their father. If I agree to any amendments, I would be accepting the need for me to be 'restrained'. That is not acceptable to me. I don't want an amendment to something that should not exist. It has been a long time since I saw my children, and if I have to, I'll wait a few more days and argue this in court.

Saturday, eleven o'clock

Another weekend. A long weekend. With no developments.

I had a cup of coffee on the deck with Taroo to keep her company. She's so sad and lonely. The poor dog is also a victim of our brutality. As I sat there, keeping her company, I noticed there was something different. I realised that Sarah has been here. Whilst I've been away at work, she has come over and taken every fucking potted and hanging plant in the garden. *Every* fucking plant on the deck, under the deck, hanging on trees . . . She's just stripped the joint whilst I wasn't here. She's such a fucking cunt. She knows me well and strikes when I'm undefended. She's a pig and a cunt.

Tuesday, at work

I have my office door locked. I'm trapped inside my room. The guys have been asking about Sarah. They've noticed that she hasn't been in, and I've had to tell them. Most cannot believe that this is the end. My people are being unexpectedly supportive. They are going about their business without hassling me. Showing their support by continuing to do business, not bothering me, keeping our business afloat.

Thursday morning

Last night, I made love to a bottle of scotch whilst watching a 'gangsters' movie where the only female lead was a mole. There was lots of violence and no women.

Today I'm very nervous. I have to go to court to get the restraining orders revoked. Jake has told me that her solicitor claims that she will not be attending the hearing. As such, he believes that it will not be necessary for him to represent me because the revocation is simply a formality. As it is not being contested, he has asked me to simply ask the magistrate that the orders be revoked. I'm very, very nervous. I hate courts. They intimidate me. They are not about justice. They are about rules. And this is more important than losing a few thousand dollars. It's about my family.

Thursday afternoon

The hearing did not go as expected. Jake's advice was wrong. The magistrate said that he would not have it annulled, that he would 'take evidence'. When I explained that I was unprepared, that I was unrepresented, that I'd expected the orders lifted, he said that if I wanted, I could defer the hearing. I was completely at a loss as to what to do, completely unprepared for this. If I went on and failed, he would enforce the orders. If delayed, it would again be weeks before I could see my children. If I proceeded alone, I could take a tumble. I was uncertain, unfamiliar, intimidated, and vulnerable. I asked him what I would have to do to prove that I'm not a monster.

He said, 'Just give me your story, and if I believe you, I'll revoke the orders. If not, I'll confirm them.'

Bastard! *You*, who has the power to determine whether or not I see my children. *You* are going to judge me. If *you* believe me. How can I convince you that I love my children? That I *need* to see them as they need to see me? How could I be credible? Sincere?

I was a mess. I told him about things as I best could. He had a statement from Sarah with her allegations against me. She claimed I had pushed her face into the mattress and that she couldn't breathe and that I'd said I was going to kill her and all sorts of horrible things. I broke down, cried again in front of strangers. I told him it was all bullshit and that I wanted to see my children, that I would not do anything that prejudiced my relationship with them, that even in my state, I would not do anything stupid. He said that even if he lifted the order, I would have to be careful in my dealings with my wife etc.

I said, 'I want to see my children. Only my children. If she doesn't want to see me, then I don't want to see her.'

In any case, after a while, I convinced him that I wasn't an animal, and he lifted the restraint on all the children and also on her. Not that I want to see her anyway, but the mere enforcement of a 'restraining order' is repulsive to me. A matter of great shame. Also, if I came across her by accident, she would have me charged. The dynamics of access would be very difficult if the restraint on Sarah was still in force.

With a little luck, I should be able to see the children this weekend.

Tape 5

First Visit of Children

Friday afternoon

It is arranged. I can see the children. She still can't bear to see me, so we are dealing through intermediaries. Robin and Laura have agreed to be the drop-off point. I am to pick them up from their house at five thirty on Saturday and drop them off again on Sunday afternoon at 4:00 p.m.

Saturday evening

My children are with me. They are now asleep. I picked them up from Robin's place and brought them back 'home'. A home that is empty. My father was at home, waiting for their arrival. He was so happy to see them and they him. We cooked dinner together. We had minestrone, and they helped me prepare it. They watched a video whilst it was cooking. We had tortilla with the minestrone and a chocolate ice cream, and afterward, they went to bed. They went to bed quite late. We stayed up and talked. I told them a story about when my family migrated to Australia on a ship called the *Aurelia*. It took ages to decide how we were going to sleep. I had to pull the mattress from my bed. They are all sleeping together on my mattress on the floor. My father has lent me some bedding we are using. They think it's fun for us all to sleep together. God, they're wonderful children.

Sunday

This morning, they woke me up. I was very tired. We had a rough and tumble on the big bed. Yesterday, when they first got here, they ran around with Taroo. Taroo was over the moon. This morning, we walked Taroo over to my father's place, had churros for breakfast there, and walked back with Taroo.

We came back, looked at rocks, shot arrows with my bow, and then I picked up my father, and we went to the zoo. It was very busy. We had to wait in line for probably forty minutes before we got in. Yayi had to go to the toilet a number of times – prostrate problems – and he got lost. So we lost him for thirty to forty minutes. Four per cent of my total time with my children, including sleep. I was angry with him because I have less than twenty-three hours with them. Time is so precious. I felt he wasted some. We walked around everywhere and had a good day. We had lunch there, and then I dropped them off at Laura's place. They were swimming when I left. That's it.

When I went to pick them up, I was a little nervous, not knowing how they would react to seeing me after all this time. I drove around for a while in the area to make sure that I wasn't early and crossed Sarah's path. I drove in after seeing her car drive away.

Robin was cheerful and helpful. As I climbed the stairs to the first floor, Jessica was at the top landing. She immediately screamed with joy, 'Daddy!' and ran down to hug me. I felt like a jellyfish, wobbly. She's so pretty. She looks a little thin, not eating. The other two were in the bath. I was glad that I had seen Jessica first. She's more spontaneous, expresses her love more easily than the other two. Claudia, wise Claudia, is more reserved. Ben, too young and uncertain.

Jessica grabbed me by the hand and dragged me to the bathroom to see her brother and sister. 'Daddy's here.' Her joy was infectious, and the other two rushed to me. I tried not to cry. I didn't succeed. After initial reservation, Claudia became a chatterbox, which is great, normal. I took them away almost immediately. On the way home, Jessica sang, 'Swans swim in the pond. Looking for fish . . . in the water . . . ahte ahte . . .' at my request. I came straight home. Yayi was here. Thank god I did not have to return to an empty house.

Sunday night

I'm home after dropping the children off. Dropping them off tears me apart. I'm in the pits of depression again. They are such lovely children. So understanding, enthusiastic, loving. They seem to be coping quite well. I'm very glad for that. But I'm also a little disappointed that they are coping so well without me. They probably miss me a little bit . . . but not . . . They seem . . . Life is going on for them. They're doing OK. They're going about their business, and everything is normal for them – sort of . . . If Sarah had not been around, if things had been reversed, would they have been worse off? It hurts me that I'm so redundant. So disposable. The near-absent father is easily adapted to weekend father. Only partially important. Disposable man.

I've been able to piece together a few things. The first night they stayed away, they were in a place where there were lots of people. They were all in one room together. I guess that was a women's refuge type of place. After that, they went to Susie's grandparents' house and stayed there for a little while. That fat bitch who claimed not to know where she was and didn't want to get involved. I will never forgive her. The snake. She's just a fat pig. I wonder what discussions they had about me without me knowing. Look at her life and her man. They are low-life, crippled, self-conscious, inhibited nobodies. Anal-retentive worms. And they have been able to affect my life, my family.

Anyway, they stayed there for about a week, I think, and after that, they went and stayed with Dianne and her husband out Bullsbrook way. My children are calling them Aunty Dianne and Uncle whatever-his-fucking-name-is. They call some strangers 'uncle' and 'aunty'.

They're such good kids. They stayed with Aunt Diane and Uncle Buggerlugs for a little while.

Her explanation to them as to why she's taken them from me was that she didn't like my disciplining of the kids. She just took them. 'I'm going to take them. I looked after them. Fuck you. They're mine.'

Fuck *you*. They're mine too. Who gives you the right to do this?

I feel as if she's cut off my balls. Cut to the core of my life.

I had a good time with the children. Despite my bitching, my father helped. I needed a win with my children. They had a good time and were pleased to see me. But it hurts. It's all so contrived. I had to ensure that they did have a good time, that their time with me was positive. It's just so forced. This woman has killed me. I would prefer to be dead. I want to be dead. My life can never be better than it has been. I can overcome and compensate, carry on. But there will never be the wholeness of me with my children and my wife in what was once a happy family. That which I hoped to be my destiny, which I could not see otherwise, is not my fate. And I feel empty. Throughout the difficult times I faced, I was . . . happy. I felt I could face anything because I had the comfort of my family. I could lose everything, and though a setback, I could cope because I was with my own, a part of a larger thing called family. My family was important. I was happy with my love of my children and with Sarah. I don't believe things can ever be better than they were at that time. That is lost to me.

And so I really do think that death is preferable. It is not anger at anyone but a realisation of the emptiness that is . . . that is in me. The uselessness of a family-less father. Compensations are not enough. Loneliness and purposelessness are my constant companions, leaving me only when I dull my senses with alcohol or drugs. I'm hollow. By my own value system, I am a failure. I have failed in my most important purpose . . . I have failed to keep my family together. I've failed to have my children with me, to provide them with the upbringing that I know is best for them. I've failed to see my children grow up. And I've failed to be able to be there when they will need me. To only see them on weekends . . . I feel sad. Nothing will compensate for my loss, my failure. I will have to make lots of changes to accommodate my new circumstances. And in doing so, I'll change. I'm afraid of what I will become. Compensation for the loss of that which I know to be the things I value most. It divides me, breaks me.

So I go on from day to day. I couldn't deny my children seeing me on the weekends. If I'm not around all the time, I can still be around for them on the weekend . . . I think it's horrible. My life is horrible. I hate what is happening. I'm dead. Dead inside. It just hurts. I've got no escape. I have to keep on with this torture.

Monday, lunchtime

I've just been home to collect a couple of things. I'm on my way back to the office. I feel a little better than I did yesterday. Last night was bad.

I discovered where she lives. She left me a note to tell me that I should change my HBF insurance from family to single. I rang to do so, and the fellow wanted to confirm a few details with me. In doing so, he confirmed my address as 36 Longwait Drive, Sorrento. I've never lived there, so it must be her new address.

I'm not going to rush over there to see her or anything like that. She doesn't want to see me, and I don't want to see her. It's still puzzling – the finality, brutality, and speed, without a word to me. No contact other than through solicitors. I'm very sorry that I'm being denied the small things of my children growing up. I used to play 'bum drum' and 'belly piano' with them. Gone. She has stolen from me my seeing our children grow. I'm not sure how to cope. I'm taking one day at a time.

I'm still very tender when it comes to my children. Whereas towards Sarah, I feel . . . What do I feel? I feel hatred. There's an element of hatred, an element of disappointment . . . ah, pity . . . for her . . . But above all, the sense of loss of what we had, that's gone, and whilst I doubt that it can be rekindled now – it may be – I doubt it. I think she was such a cunt for doing this to me, to our family. In such a nasty way. Our future no longer exists. Only a few weeks ago, we had a past, a present, and a future. Now there's only a past. The past, which was a joy for the future, has now become painful memories. Yesterday I had a past. Today that past burns me. There is no future.

Last night, I had a call from Susan Bernstein. Sarah has spoken to her, and she gave me a call. I didn't go into details with her. I didn't have any explanations because I still don't know how this could have happened. She called me to see how I was coping. It was nice of Susan to show concern and call.

The restraining order, lack of contact, forced sole custody, solicitors, not speaking and not writing. Fuck.

Afternoon

Watching television hurts. The 'international year of the family' hurts. Seeing fathers walking with their children hurts. Seeing families together hurts.

I hate my wife for destroying my family. This issue of the restraining order is unjust. She could go there and claim anything, and because I'm not there to defend it, there is an interim order against me. Immediately, I am in a defensive position. I'm prevented from seeing my children, and there is a question mark against me. I was guilty, and I had to prove my innocence. It sucks.

On the strength of hearsay from one party, a father is prevented from seeing his children. Sure, there are all sorts of animals in this world who beat and abuse the innocent. These innocent victims need protection. But rather than an 'interim order' that is one to two months long, why not 'OK, victim, what you say may be true, so I'll see you and the accused here in . . . say, one week'? Maximum of one week. Then if proved, as long as required. But not two months on the strength of what one person claims the other has done. No wonder some men commit such horrible acts under these circumstances

This system is abused. Restraints are used as 'tactical weapons' to take the initiative, the advantage. 'I've got the kids. You are an animal and need restraining. Now come and take them from me.' You enter the ring to fight for your family and your children with hands tied. You cannot delay. Time works against you. Your mind is racing, in a panic. The brutal tactic demands its toll. It's in a hurry.

Sunday, the following week

I'm home after dropping off the children again. Doom is again upon me.

The tape has been faulty, and I haven't had a chance to speak to you for a while.

We had a nice weekend. There was less pressure this weekend. Yesterday I brought them back home, and they watched a video while I cooked. We had a lovely dinner. They were all very chatty and enjoyed it. They were loving and open. Sleeping was great. Sleeping all in one bed was fun. This morning, we had breakfast slowly, and afterward, we played. We were on Ben's bike and took turns rolling down the steep driveway. Ben fearlessly letting go, feet up in the air, tearing along. Claudia and Jessica were a little shy. They would only start from about two-thirds up. Gradually, they took off from higher and higher up the driveway until they were starting from up the top. I was going down too.

We visited Yayi, and we all came back here and had lunch. Afterward, I told my father to go. He was hurt at first. I was a little angry that in my twenty-two hours of fathering, he is always around. I explained that I needed time alone with my children. He is their grandfather. They need him, and he needs them as well. But the twenty-two hours I get have to be shared with my father. It's not enough. I don't want to deny him his grandchildren. I would like for him to see them as much as possible. But I do need for my children to see *me* alone, for them to recognise *me* rather than just half of a couple, first with Sarah and now with my father. He understood and was gracious on departure. I'm a little jealous of my children's affection towards my father.

We went to the museum and looked at the giant whale. They enjoyed themselves. There was less pressure. We had an ice cream al fresco in one of the cafés in James Street. They show such appreciation over the smallest thing. They're such lovely kids. They are really lovely. I dropped them off at Laura's, and now I'm home again.

The clouds have returned. I always feel fucking horrible on Sundays. At this time. I miss them already. I'm going to be alone all week . . . again.

It's horrible. I feel lousy. I asked them to ring me through the week. Ben rings Yayi. He misses Yayi. He doesn't ring *me*. He doesn't miss *me*. This is worse than death.

Ben has learnt the word 'escaped'. Last night, he mentioned that Mummy had escaped from here. 'Mummy had *escaped* from here.' It hurt. She escaped from here. She escaped from me, an animal.

I hope they ring me through the week. I try to have a good time with them without being too depressed or false. It is such a short time. There is always the pressure to get them back on time.

This stage is horrible. Jake was right. I am going through the worst period of my life. I still don't understand. I'm still confused. My feelings towards Sarah are always changing. Sometimes I hope that things could be as they used to be. That's impossible. There is regret, sorrow, and blame.

With my children, I feel cheated. Injustice that I don't have them. I'm sorry I don't have them longer. I believe Claudia and Jessica also think so. Jessica would probably prefer to live with me. They all would, except for Ben. He's so young. It's so wrong. Eventually, it will stop hurting. We'll grow apart, get used to seeing one another on the weekends only. It's so unnatural. To get used to being a once-a-week . . . a 'sometimes' father. I don't know what sort of father I can be only on weekends.

I think I was a good father. Now I'm a dismissed father. Disposable.

It's been six and a half weeks. Six and a half weeks. Six weeks of my life.

Tuesday

I'm having a bad day again today. Yesterday I had another shit day. At work, I tried, not too convincingly, to look busy, but I achieved very little. Today I went to a conciliation meeting at the chamber over a dispute with another firm, and I was half effective at best. Normally, I would have been much better. Better prepared, tougher. I would have probably won. It looks as if I'll lose that one.

I'm feeling lousy again today. I have a gut ache that hurts all the way down to my toes. I'm still in love with Sarah. I wish I wasn't. I know myself well enough to realise I could not forgive this. It will always stand between us. I'm not sure what her position is anyway, but I miss her.

Normally, I would take an opportunity like this, being alone, to go out drinking etc. I would have thought that given this opportunity, I would be out whoring. But now that I am free to fulfil my fantasies, my heart is not in it. I'm incredibly lonely, yet I don't want to do anything to stop me being lonely. I'm working through these feelings in the hope that I can purge myself more quickly. But at the moment, I'm suffering. I'm in the car, driving around aimlessly because I had to get out of the office.

God, how I wish she would contact me. We could at least talk to each other, and I could find out what went wrong. Normal. Just normalise things. Doubt is so painful. Uncertainty. The loss of my children. I'm going to go broke. Business is tough, legal costs. Refinancing two properties is not helping. We are going through a bit of a trough, and this also is pressure. Borderline.

I turn a corner and hope that Sarah's car is in the driveway.

I went to my shrink today for a session. He feels that I'm coping remarkably well under the circumstances. My tape recorder friend, you have helped. My wife has vanished from my life. Comparing it to someone dying, at least you can reconcile yourself with losing a person that you loved and who loved you, as opposed to this situation, where someone you love vanishes – worse, who can, at their will, contact you but doesn't. There are many issues that hurt, but I feel that one of the most painful is not knowing. Not being able to talk through it or away.

My shrink says that there is a danger in me thinking that I'm such a horrible person that the person I most love can't stand being near me. They fear me. He worries about the resulting effect on my personal esteem. Self-love can be destroyed. That is probably at play, though I don't think that I'm such a monster. I haven't allowed myself. I'm not. I'm not a horrible person. I don't know what's happened, but it can't be entirely *my* fault.

He mentioned another possibility that Sarah may have intellectually made up her mind to break but that her feelings are different. The denial is there to enforce her mental resolution, which may be betrayed by her feelings. If she were to see me, she could weaken her resolve.

I tend to lean more towards the second possibility.

He mentioned that at some stage in the future, I'm going to have to forgive her. Otherwise, I won't grow. Grow? What does he mean? He says that for my own sake, I'll have to forgive her. I don't know how I am going to be able to do that. By my system of values, neither the method nor the act are justifiable. Particularly the method. How can I forgive? How do I let this go?

I haven't spoken to my tape recorder as often lately. The tape recorder has been useful in talking about my feelings, working them out. Lately, rather than being immersed in my feelings, I have been on 'feeling block-out'. Trying to deal with things by trying to block out the pain may not be so helpful, but it buys me time. I'm on drugs. The psyche has prescribed me Zoloft. At the moment, I'm on overload and cannot deal with everything that's on my plate. So, I block out my feelings in the hope that some of these issues will sort themselves out on their own. In time, I'll have to front the new me, but I'm not strong enough yet. Block-out doesn't allow me to release. I'm pushing my problems into the future. But that is the best I can do for the moment.

Since Sunday, things have been shaky. On Sunday afternoon/night, I was a mess. On Monday, I was ineffective. Tuesday was the same. Today is Wednesday.

Going to the psycho helps. I think I need to talk. It is good to talk to another human. I also need to talk to you, tape recorder, to talk out these feelings. Otherwise, it becomes a clogging fear, a stomach ache that combines sadness, anxiety, and powerlessness.

Monday morning,

Mondays are always horrible. The day after I return the children. Through the week, I do things to keep busy. By Wednesday/Thursday, I forget how lonely I am. On Friday, I start looking forward to my children's visit. On Saturday morning, I'm expectant. Then by Sunday lunchtime, I start feeling the pressure of having to take them back. Sunday late afternoon/ evening is the pits. Their presence reminds me how lonely I am.

This week, again, there was a problem with access. It was Pam's birthday. Laura and Robin took her to Adventure World and did not return in time. I waited around, and finally, at five thirty, I got a phone call to tell me that I could collect them at six thirty. An hour less out of my time. So it was rush, rush, and rush.

Sunday, I felt I had failed them a little because my present for Claudia's birthday, the kite, didn't fly. I tried it on two separate occasions, and it didn't fly. My darling daughter's first birthday without me. My present to her didn't fly.

We then went to the Museum for Children, and it was closed. We didn't have time for an ice cream.

Last week, I was busy. I went to see a rock-and-roll band on Wednesday. I saw Atomic Swing. That was really good. It was good to forget. There was a young girl there who fancied me, and that was nice – an ego boost. On Thursday, I went sailing. A relaxing twilight sail with experienced sailors – social yet competitive. I met a woman there who seems interested in me and gave me her phone number so I can contact her. There is a little crescendo on the female front. On Friday, I was going to go home after work, but Al insisted I go out with him and Marc. They took me to a place where the 'raunchy girls' were performing. Al claims he arranged it. He probably did. One of these girls got me out and sat on my chest, and another wiggled her derriere on my cock. I found it humiliating, didn't like it at all. I pretended to have fun. Afterward, we went to a nightclub.

The body has its own timetable; whilst my mind is tortured with self-doubt, my cock drives me on.

I was a bit buggered on Saturday. I'm trying to get used to being alone, socialising as a single man. Expensive – women still don't pay their share. Perverse equality. On Friday, I took out Donna for Secretary's Day. That was exciting.

The weekend with the children was a joy. Then Sunday night came. I went to bed as soon as I got home from taking them back so as not to descend to doom. When I awoke, I paced around with nothing to do. I decided to go to the movies. I went to see *Schindler's List* alone. A mistake. I cried at the movies.

I'm ineffective at work. This morning, I held a sales meeting, watched a video, etc., and now I'm shopping. I'm doing Sarah's work, not mine. I'm ineffective, and I don't care.

TAPE 6

Sarah and I Meet

Tuesday

Last night, I got a note from Sarah, the first note I've had. I rang Robin and asked him whether he thought it was wise for me to go see her. He advised me to do so. I went to see her. As I walked up the stairs to her front door, I could hear Ben throwing a fit. I knocked.

Without opening, she asked, 'Who is it?'

'Me.'

'I don't want to see you.'

'I want to see you, Sarah. Please.'

'No, no, not now.'

'What about in half an hour?'

'OK then. In an hour.'

I went to a nearby park and planned what I would say as I waited for the hour to pass. I returned after an hour. I didn't know how to start, what to say. She didn't let me in. We stayed outside and talked. It wasn't what I'd hoped, but at least we talked. She mentioned that she'd lost feeling, not only for me but all feeling. She was numb and didn't know what to feel. She didn't like what she'd become. She said she had to do what she did. She said the restraining orders were to buy some space. That she knew I would be looking for her, coming after her.

She claimed three problems with me. Uncontrollable anger. That there was this 'dark side' to me and that she believes I don't love her because I can't love myself. I've thought about what she said and don't agree. I do show anger easily, but it is never 'uncontrolled'. I always see me in my anger and watch me in anger to ensure that I do not lose control. In fact, when I'm angriest, I'm silent. Cold anger is worse, and that would never be 'uncontrolled'. The 'dark side' of me . . . yes, there is. There is a dark side to me, but so too is there a dark side to everyone. I live with mine. I hide when the beast is on the prowl. The business about not loving her because I don't love myself is a lot of horseshit and more to do with present sociological fashion. Psychology from Corn Flakes packets. That I don't love myself, I don't agree with at all. I'm comfortable with myself. I like me, and I have a reasonable amount of self-esteem. I'm comfortable with my lot. I don't accept her view. I *am* capable of love.

It was good that we talked. Again, she got something out of me. I'm going to let her take the children away to a holiday house we'd booked for the family a few months ago. She'll be there for over a week, so it will mean I will miss my access on one weekend. This will result in a period of two weeks between visits. We agreed that I would have them an extra day during the Easter break.

In return, she has agreed to help me tie up a few loose ends with the work she left. She'll ring me. It was constructive though. She wouldn't look at me. She wouldn't let me touch her. We sat outside her front door.

Sarah had said that I was always depressed. This is bullshit. I'm generally positive. I think I'm one of the most cheerful characters I know. I'm able to remain cheerful under circumstances that would drive most people to

---

insanity. To see the 'silver lining' in the darkest of clouds. Her reflection must have been very dark indeed.

Two weeks later

Tape recorder, I need you less. It's been a long time since I shared my secrets with you. I need you today.

It is two months and three days since Sarah left me, and I'm having a lousy day. I've stopped taking the medication that the doctor prescribed to me. Whilst it helped me block out, it was only putting things off. I wasn't feeling enough, going about from day to day in a cheery numbness. I decided to try life without drugs to see if I am strong enough. I want to go through this in full awareness. I stopped the drugs, and as a consequence, the clouds have returned, and I'm not well. I wasn't coping. The drugs were.

Sunday afternoon

Sarah came to collect the children. I hate Sunday afternoons. She wants me to transfer registration of her car away from the business to her. It wasn't a good weekend. Maybe we didn't do enough. Maybe the children were bored. It was hard, fucking hard.

As they drove away, it was I who waved at them from my bedroom window. It tears at me as my family is torn, broken. Just prior to driving away, whilst the kids were in the car, Sarah walked back to me to hand me a letter. She told me to read it after she left.

'No, no! Wait on. I'll have a look at it.'

It was just another nasty, bitchy note. It talked about the car and that she was going to break off relations and other threats.

'Look, let's talk.'

So we talked a while, and she got angry and left mid-sentence.

I rang her about half an hour later, and we talked for quite a long time. Again, it was dreadful. She claimed eighteen years of abuse underpinned by the threat of violence, weapons everywhere. That . . . that's what she remembers. She said the children were better off without me. That Claudia was more relaxed, Jessica was sleeping better.

What violence? My weapons around the house. Sticks and swords. I train with them. I teach martial arts, for Christ's sake. Of course, I have weapons. It's what I do.

She knows how to hurt me. She uses the children against me. The children are not better off without me. Jessica is not eating. She looks very thin. Ben cries when she drops them off, 'I want Mummy!' and when she picks them up, 'I want Daddy!' What kind of upbringing will my children have without me? 'Que vida de miseria.' Bitch! She tries to paint me into a corner. I'm not a monster. I was trying to talk. To talk! Trying to build bridges. But each time we see each other, there is more distance. I signed over the car to her and dropped off the papers at once.

I went to my shrink. He says that I should not surrender, to not concede everything, give up. That isn't real and wouldn't work. That I have to hold something back for me. I agree. But every time I'm with her, a huge variety of emotions struggle for supremacy in my being. Turn the clock back. Things are a shithouse. When I come away from her, a difference in me reasserts itself.

I wrote her a letter, which I haven't given to her. I don't know if I will. It talked about how her accusations hurt and that we must have lived in different marriages. I don't recognise myself as she described me. I don't believe this to be me. It is not true, but she sees me differently.

I thought of her as my friend, a person that knew me, which I could relate to and trust. Someone with similar goals, common approaches, common values. All that was a fantasy. Not true. It didn't exist for her, and it really wasn't true for me. She told me that she'd written me a letter after an argument more than a year ago. She was going to leave me then. She had put it off, hoping for a change of heart. She had never given it to me, but every month she would pull it out and read it. Unbeknown to me, our relationship was finished. We were dead a year earlier, but the corpse had yet to be buried.

In my letter to her, I explained that under those circumstances, our marriage was over a year ago. Her private reading of her letter so many times was simply an affirmation of her hatred for me. Under those circumstances, every action of mine, everything I did, would have been absolutely repulsive. She hated me. In that environment of criticism, of looking at someone with disgust, there was no room for us. When she ceased to love me, my every action must have been unbearable. I still love her, I think. She hasn't loved me for a very long time.

I don't know how to cope with being without the children. How has their opinion of me been perverted by her repulsion of me? They are suffering because of her denial and delusion. Poor little bastards. She bottled her disgust of me for so long, the end was inevitable, and when it came, it came in an explosion of brutality and blame.

I hate her as much as love her. I can't trust her. I don't know what to do or how to best help my children. They're different now. They're without a father around and not part of a family.

Should I persist? Continue to work at this, try to bridge? Such a long fucking bridge, with shaky foundations. Can the horror of recent times be forgiven or forgotten? If our love is dead, why can't I bury it? Why must I endure its putrid stench?

If my children are, as she accuses, better off without me, how do I live with that? How? When I thought I was a good father? All my beliefs are crumbling. I don't know what to do. I'm really in a mess . . . today.

Everything seems so futile. We could have done so much and didn't. Everywhere I look, I see failure. Everything I've done is a failure. I have failed in my marriage. I've made too many mad, wrong decisions, business is shithouse, and . . . everything is fucking terrible.

Monday

I'm driving around with my sunglasses on so no one can see me. I caught a glimpse of myself in the rear-view mirror, and I look as bad as I feel. It's all a charade. Nothing is right. I'm going to have to go back on medication. Block out. I can't live like this. I've tried and can't cope. I hope drugs make me a happy idiot. I know it is not real, hiding from reality. This is real. Pain is real. These are my true feelings, but I'm not able to cope with my feelings. I need to block them out with drugs to buy time. 'Time heals all wounds.' I fucking hope so.

Failure, failure at anything that matters, stares accusingly at me.

I had a look at a house in Coolbinia. It was a really attractive house with curved glass on Armadillo Crescent. It is badly damaged, needing of lots of repair, broken windows, etc. I thought that if I stretched and put an offer on it . . . I was so excited . . . It was the house we'd always wanted. I was going to drive over to Sarah and drag her over to see it. No! No! An illusion. I'm deluding myself. I was excited that if I bought the house of our dreams . . . our dreams . . . ha! Is there, was there ever such a thing?

What a fucking loser! Buy a house, and the family is thrown in. What a fucking joke.

Monday night

I've just got back from dinner with Sarah and the children. As arranged, she came in to tidy up loose ends at work. She was late. Instead of five thirty, she came in at six fifteen. We went to a Chinese restaurant. It didn't quite work out. Just horrible. With the kids there. They were so good, expectant. Nervous, tense.

At the end of it, I handed her the letter. I was uncertain as to whether or not I would give it to her. I decided that I needed some specific feedback from her. She took it, said goodbye. I kissed the children. The clouds hung over us throughout the night. I remember going out to dinner with the kids as a family. This is not it. This is not it. What is my role in this? It shows, highlights, how far we've fallen. Such distance. We don't understand one another.

I don't feel like doing anything. I feel like crawling into a hole. I'll bleed some more. Harden the scar and wound.

Sarah,

How far have we come?

Just a few weeks ago, you were an integral part of me. You knew my every thought. We were one.

I suppose the reality is that I have not accepted that you have left me. Regardless of the game play, how I tried to cope with the situation or what I have said to you, to myself, or to anyone else, I still hoped that you and I would be able to repair our marriage and continue our life together. I have felt that to be the best option for the children, for me and for you. Whilst I'm uncertain about many things at present, I believe very strongly that a dual-parent family provides the best environment in which the children can develop.

Anything else, I believe, falls far short of that and would only be contemplated if the benefits were well outweighed by other problems (huge and permanent). As such, I have been trying to accommodate your needs as much as I can whilst largely suppressing mine.

Quite frankly, I had hoped, believed, that your ultimate goal was one of reconciliation.

I could not believe that your intentions were to terminate our marriage. Regardless of how often your solicitor, others, or you, in your many ways, told me that our marriage was over, I could not believe it. I hoped they were temporary words in anger. I am a slow learner. You know that.

I am, reluctantly and with much pain and withdrawal, coming to the realisation that reconciliation has very short odds.

The letter you wrote to me and didn't give me was a cancer. Your reading it to yourself on a regular basis affirmed the inevitability of destruction. How could I have not known that love was filtering out of you? Or maybe I did feel it and reacted to you, to your withdrawal, in a way that worsened our chances. To a large extent, since that day, we have each lived in a different marriage.

Each meeting, conversation between us ends badly. All contact results in new acts for us to forgive and forget. No doubt you feel the same. I'm still very much in love with you (for good or bad), but I'm falling out of like with you.

Seeing you, not seeing you, talking to you, or not talking to you causes me pain. I feel as if we no longer share values or goals.

I cannot continue in the present mode, with life at a standstill, full of unrealisable expectations. The present is only pain and loss with little purpose and life itself in question. I fear for me. I cannot continue in a state where my life is a failure on all fronts. This is not your problem, I know. Yet 'once upon a time', we would have tried to help one another. The 'me' has always taken precedence over the 'we', I know, but the 'we' came a very close second.

Things are different now. How far you've come away from the 'us', I don't know. But I need to know. I need to know from you in real terms that you will make a commitment to our marriage that reconciliation is a priority for you. With that knowledge and commitment to 'us', we can address all issues together. I need to know that now, not in the future.

Sarah, I mean you no harm. I love you. That remains a constant. I fear that my love will turn to hate, and I don't want that to happen. I cannot live like this. I need to know.

When you left me, you made no contact with me because you felt that to be best. I resisted because I needed repair, reconciliation. Your brutality bears pragmatic sense. Minimal contact may be the best course of action if you cannot make a commitment to our marriage.

I fear your response, am frightened of the consequences, but I cannot go on.

As you know, I don't believe that 'absence makes the heart grow fonder'. For me, it is quite the opposite.

Without children, our separation would be easier. We would never have to see each other again. Whether that is an advantage or otherwise, time will tell. But if we are not both going to put our all into our marriage, then we should allow each other the metamorphosis of falling out of love. In honour of what once was, let us be humane.

Please call me or write to me soon, Sarah.

Your Very Confused Husband

Epiloque

Two and a half years later, I look back on the closing stages of my marriage with a sorrow that faded too slowly. I listened to my tapes for the first time recently and hoped that doing so would help to purge the past from me. I had hoped that by listening to events as they unfolded rather than through the fog of memory, I would gain the perspective of release. Instead, I get flashes of my former life in which I see myself as a bit player in my own play. Events churn along with chaotic predetermination and drag me powerlessly along.

Agony slaps my face and squeezes my throat as I watch my character behaving in a repulsive manner. I am deeply ashamed of some of my actions. I see trivial matters blown out of proportion, power struggles between us, mainly over control of the children's upbringing. Powerlessness, fear, and a sense of inadequacy at being unable to provide the environment I had hoped, continue to burden me. I see moody detachment when I felt wronged and psychological cruelty as payback. All of this sometimes peppered with a meanness of spirit I had not recognised. If only . . .

We were on a one-way track to destruction. I wish I had been able to step back and look at our lives as it was. Maybe then, I could have seen the cancer that destroyed Sarah's love for me. She meant everything to me. At the time, I could not see how many problems plagued our relationship. They should have been obvious to me, but they were not. I suppressed my feelings and pushed on. The responsibility of supporting our family made introspection a luxury I could not afford. I was under so much pressure, being responsible for five people, that I didn't have time for the space to assess how I felt about things and where we were going. The burden of support enslaved me. I was on feeling repression. I blocked out the fear of failure and economic uncertainty, and I built a shield to protect me from the brutalities of business failures. In doing so, I also lost sensitivity to those I love. I threw the baby out with the bathwater. I had become a hard man at work, and regrettably, some of it came home with me. I now feel that I was a prisoner to the chains of protector/provider. No doubt there are many other men in exactly the same trap, caught by their need to be wanted, playing out a predestined role of provider and, in doing so, alienating those for whom they sacrifice their time, their energy, and ultimately, their lives.

I could have continued in that mode for a long time, maybe forever, but Sarah pulled the plug on our relationship. It saddens me to know that we have so little to show for our eighteen years together.

The anxiety of loss seems to reside in my solar plexus. It feels concrete, physical. I can almost touch it. It feels like a pulsating puss. At times I feel like plunging a knife into my chest to open the wound and allow the putrid pus to ooze out of me. Piercing the wound would release me. I feel that if the disease residing inside my solar plexus could be pierced and the pus cleaned, my pain would stop. My pain is tangible, alive, concentrated. It watches me as I make these notes, pulsing, pulling.

Fear, pain, and doubt remain millimetres from the surface. I live on a knife's edge of anxiety, surviving by block-out, immobilised by fear and a lack of purpose.

When does the pain stop? When does it stop?

Is this pain part of the rebirth? Will this pain result in a metamorphosis into a new me? And if that is so, how can there be rebirth if one has memory? There cannot be a true rebirth if one has memory. Memory will remind you of what once was and poison the present. I remember a rostrum talk in which I said that I am all my previous mes, each exerting unequal influence on the present me. The me that is broken is all powerful. The old me will always exist.

It is fashionable to talk of letting go. What does letting go mean? I don't understand how to let go of something that is so me. To let go seems to me to be about becoming someone else, and I am trapped in me. If this is the only release from pain, how do I do it? Do I try to override memory and forget? Is the loss of memory the key? If so, how do I forget? I don't know how letting go is possible. Memory prevents me from letting go. I wish I could. I have yet to know what letting go means and how to do it.

If there is no letting go, if I am not able to 'let go', what room is there for anyone else? What is there of value in me for someone else? Why would anyone want to deal with someone who is so damaged? Does one lower expectations of relationships? Do I demand or expect less of anyone else? Am I then more prepared to accept more of a compromise? Is acceptance of less than you've known part of maturity, or if not, do I continue without purpose or significant connection other than duty and obligation? I hope I can bleach the pain from my memories, enough to allow me to function with less regret.

Renée Geyer screams at me, 'If loving you is wrong, I don't want to be right!'

Love is an impostor. It does not exist in the way it appears. It is deceitful and contrives to take on the shape of other feelings, such as tenderness, lust, despair, dependence, and so on. By the time you arrive at love itself, its object has vanished. I look at young lovers with envy. I do not envy their love. I envy their naivety. I envy their capacity to live the illusion of love.

I have forgiven Sarah. It's arisen slowly over a long period. Nevertheless, I do not trust her. Having known her capacity for betrayal and self-preservation, I am aware that she would burn me if I stand in the way of any of her objectives or values. Empathy was never one of her qualities. Now even though our relationship is quite cordial, whenever she makes an unexpected move or asks for something, I feel compelled to analyse it to establish if there is a hidden agenda and to ascertain if my response can do me harm. I still feel vulnerable. I'm forever watchful of the possible harm that she can do me. We conduct our affairs in as friendly a manner as possible, trying to avoid triggers that immediately take us back to the horrors of the past, with its associated hostility and distrust. Hostility is very near to the surface and will escape its cage over what, to others, would appear quite insignificant. Our hostility has been papered over but runs very deep. I am in awe of its power and its readiness to resurface and join the battle for no obvious reason.

I remain disappointed that someone who was to be a life partner could behave in such a way. 'Through thick and thin.' It was obviously too thick or too thin. One reserves the greatest resentment for those to whom one confides one's trust, exposes their vulnerabilities, and who betray one's trust. The greater the love, the higher the hate. No one has hurt me as she has. I cannot let anyone else hurt me in the same way ever again.

I am still trying to forgive myself. After all this time, I haven't quite forgiven myself for having lost my family. I continue to blame myself for the many errors I committed. The responsibility for the collapse of my family rests heavily on my shoulders. Regardless of the reasons for such a loss, I feel a failure. I was born to be a father and have failed.

How can I forgive the assassin that entered my soul and consumed it? I must forgive myself. I must forgive my failure, my incapacity to hold on to that which I treasured most in life. Hopefully, in time, I can. But I haven't yet.

I am accustomed to my present life – more outings, infrequent sexual encounters, loads of alcohol, living alone. In times past, I might have looked at my present consequences with envy or, at least, less contempt. My present 'freedom' may have once appeared attractive. Superficially, it is entertaining. I am able to do much that I was not able to do before.

But my core remains deeply sad. I remain hollow.

Grieving has not released me from the pain which surfaces unpredictably, triggered by the apparently trivial. My sense of aloneness has resurfaced with a vengeance. These recordings have taken me back to a very dark place in my past, full of pain and regret. I have many acquaintances, socialise in a wide variety of circles. I am popular and reasonably attractive. I am attracted to and attract women of varying ages, experience, and education. But no one comes close. No one connects in more than a limited way. I interact in variety, using different people to fulfil different needs. My soul bellows, 'Damaged goods!'

I have established a wide circle of friends. This took some time as I felt out of synch with many of the friends I shared with my former wife. As she gained custody of our children, she also gained custody of many of our previous friends. I felt disenfranchised from friends with whom we socialised as a family. She was better able to retain those. Also, with my having conceded the role of 'social director' in our family to Sarah, she had greater experience at connecting with our friends. She got custody of my children and friends.

Establishing a new social network was quite slow and difficult. Initially, many of those contacts were new and relevant only to my role as a single man. In time, I was able to reconnect with some of my former friends who were able to deal with the new me. Couples, friends of a single man.

Yet I maintain a life of solitude and emptiness sprinkled with material distractions and sexual fantasies. I long not only for events of the past but also for my past's future. My past had a future. My present lacks a sense of future. I live for now and feel the emptiness of a tomorrow that has no sense of itself.

Periodically, I get a surge of energy with which I hope to crash through the pain. But it is illusionary and fades well before I have found meaning. Doubt sponges my energy. Energy disappears.

Two and a half years seems such a long time. Much has happened. I am older, look younger or at least more marketable. My life's schedule has undergone much change. My life provides me with some joy. I am learning to appreciate small wonders that, in the past, would have gone unnoticed. Therein may lie the answer. I don't know. I hope so.

I am still undergoing a process of self-discovery and change. The metamorphosis continues. God only knows where it will end.

I am still here.

9 781669 889182